"Your devotional]   he
smartest, strongest   nd
content being who   :ca
Friedlander provides a road map ɪoɪ ᴋᴇᴇᴘɪɴɢ ᴀ   .od
who designed you and who has great designs for your life. This
is a must-read for anyone who wants to experience God's peace,
purpose, and passion for life."

Bill Farrel, director of Proverbs 19:8 Ministries,
author of *Men Are Like Waffles, Women Are Like Spaghetti*
and *The 10 Best Decisions a Man Can Make*

"Do you ever long for a fresh approach to your relationship with
God? In this book, you'll find an insightful spiritual guide in Rebecca Friedlander. She writes with beauty that will intrigue you,
and she explains the spiritual disciplines in a way that makes you
want to dive in. If you're ready for more adventure and closeness
in your walk with Jesus, this is your book."

Arlene Pellicane, speaker and author
of *Calm, Cool, and Connected*

"Throughout history, men and women have found that the path
to intimacy with God is a journey of discovery and adventure.
This beautifully written book is personal, practical, and Christ-
centered and will greatly assist those who read it in their spiritual
journey. I believe this book will help restore the life-giving ancient
disciplines of the Church to a new generation."

Archbishop Dr. Russell McClanahan,
the Evangelical Episcopal Communion

"Rebecca Friedlander invites you to join her on the most important adventure of your life. This book will encourage you to find
and deepen your relationship with God. Rebecca can help you
find purpose in and for your life. She invites you to discover the
warmth of Someone who already loves you."

Archbishop Robert L. Wise, coauthor of *82 Days
on Okinawa* and *I Marched with Patton*

"After walking with the Lord for half a century, I've observed that it's easy for a disciple to become slightly deaf. My good friend Rebecca Friedlander blew the wax out of my ears with two words: 'Perseverance Trail.' I highly recommend her writing to anyone who wants to persevere and journey further in their discipleship with Jesus. 'But the one who endures to the end will be saved' (Matt. 24:13 CSB)."

Paul Clark, singer, songwriter, recording artist, pioneer of Christian music

"'Oh no,' you say. 'I've sworn off books on spiritual discipline for good! I've already failed at every foolproof formula for spiritual maturity I've read and I'm steering clear of any more guilt.' Good—then you're ready for this wonderful revelation that God loves you already and he's not at all surprised that you are miles from perfect spiritual maturity. He invites you to take his hand through these precious pages and walk with him as a toddler who trusts her Daddy to be with her and pick her up when she falls down. Will it hurt to learn from someone like Rebecca, who is a few steps farther down the road with the Father? Not a bit!"

Nancy Honeytree Miller, recording artist, pioneer of Christian music

THE
DIVINE
Adventure

THE
DIVINE

Adventure

SPIRITUAL PRACTICES
FOR A MODERN-DAY DISCIPLE

REBECCA FRIEDLANDER

BakerBooks
a division of Baker Publishing Group
Grand Rapids, Michigan

Published by Baker Books
a division of Baker Publishing Group
PO Box 6287, Grand Rapids, MI 49516-6287
www.bakerbooks.com

Printed in the United States of America

Library of Congress Cataloging-in-Publication Data
Names: Friedlander, Rebecca, 1980– author.
Title: The divine adventure : spiritual practices for a modern-day disciple / Rebecca Friedlander.
Description: Grand Rapids, Michigan : Baker Books, a division of Baker Publishing Group, [2021]
Identifiers: LCCN 2020051880 | ISBN 9780801093845 (paperback) | ISBN 9781540901682 (casebound) | ISBN 9781493430284 (ebook)
Subjects: LCSH: Spiritual life—Christianity.
Classification: LCC BV4501.3 .F747 2021 | DDC 248—dc23
LC record available at https://lccn.loc.gov/2020051880

Published in association with William K. Jensen Literary Agency.

21 22 23 24 25 26 27   7 6 5 4 3 2 1

To Julie,
my godmother and friend.
Thank you for praying with me
through the hills and valleys
of my divine adventure.
And for making me laugh.
I love you!

Contents

Introduction

A crisp breeze with the scent of mossy pine trees filled the air. The team of actors and film crew members emerged from their cars, ready to hike the rugged Alaskan trail. Carrying swords, leather costumes, a drone, and picnic lunches, and with medieval chain mail slung over our shoulders, we were about to shoot an epic fantasy film I had written. With a bag of cameras on my back and a set list of notes in my pocket, I excitedly pointed toward the narrow path, and we began our climb to the film location.

For months, we'd been planning for this day: writing scripts, building layers of plotlines, developing characters, and choosing a mountainous location in Juneau for the opening scene. Without a large budget, a film studio, or investors, I had simply saved my pennies to create this project. A few members of the team from Texas had even paid their own travel costs out of a personal belief in this venture. I pinched myself with excitement. Our first day of filming was finally here!

Local scouts had told me that the target destination offered a stunning mountain view, and the hiking trail was fairly straight-forward. It would be well worth the trek.

"It only takes ninety minutes to hike," they said offhandedly. "It's very easy."

Looking back, I should have known better. They were hard-core Alaskans, and the path was named Perseverance Trail. Easy? Sure . . .

A few minutes of hiking made it clear we were not prepared for the intensity of the path. We found ourselves growing weary as our feet plodded from one mountain to another. The air was thin and the blinding northern sun rose high, demanding more energy than we could possibly have imagined. Our packs felt increasingly more awkward and cumbersome as we ascended miles of winding trails through glacial forests. The crew from Alaska was loving it. The actors from Texas were dying! I peppered the conversation with pep talks, resolutely believing that our goal would be worth the grueling effort.

"We've got this," I called to my team, then gulped for air. "This is going to be incredible. Let's do this!"

Several hours later, we passed the tree line and continued through grassy alpine meadows. Exhausted, we were finally rewarded with the fantastic vista we had been anticipating: the film site for our opening scene. The thundering roar of a giant waterfall met our ears. Furiously cascading down layers of jewel-toned mountain peaks all studded with snow, it leapt over the craggy canyons with raw energy. We licked our dry lips, willing our bodies to make the last few steps, and came to rest on a plateau lined with soft grass—the icy river racing beside us. We had arrived at our film location, more beautiful than we could have imagined. It was like a set from Middle-earth—a wild paradise of raw, magnificent beauty. We fell silent . . . breathless . . . tingling with the sensation of the vivid life around us.

Our discovery of this beauty of nature was coupled with another sense of exhilaration. For me, not only was the destination worth the trek but it was the fulfillment of a dream in my heart: to create a film story that would touch lives around the world with a unique, powerful message of Christ's love. It was a thrill to be on a mission to share his heart with the world. The intense climb up Perseverance Trail to capture this story made every cell in my being tingle with wonder. Intuitively, I knew I was wrapping my fingers around the unique adventure God had designed for me, and I sensed his pleasure.

By the end of the day, we all felt brave. We forgot our burning lungs and aching feet. On the way back, the Texans even beat the Alaskans to the bottom of the mountainous trail.

In order to fully live this divine adventure, our team had to prepare for the journey. We had to make travel arrangements, create costumes, pack equipment, ship swords, plan meals, write scripts, and hike a mountain trail to arrive at the film site. The preparation wasn't the adventure, but without it, we would never have arrived at the destination.

In the same way, spiritual practices are the building blocks that help us prepare for the adventure God has waiting for each of us. The chapters in this book will help you unleash your personal journey with God, preparing and equipping you for his plan. Some of these practices offer beautiful, breathtaking vistas, while others may be a steeper climb that will challenge and stir you to greater action. Embracing your spiritual journey with Christ will exhilarate you, promising incredible, unimaginable rewards—but it may not always be easy. In fact, it will offer moments that stretch your perspective to new heights as you prepare for his plan.

You may not climb a mountain in Alaska or film sword fighters next to a waterfall, but there is something in this world that will challenge your thinking, ignite your heart, and make your soul sing. God has scripted your unique story with captivating elements of discovery, wonder, and fulfillment.

God's plan for you is amazing and unique, helping you build a solid foundation for a thriving walk with him.

Spiritual practices are the building blocks that help us prepare for the adventure God has waiting for each of us.

Beyond Normal

When I was in Sunday school as a twelve-year-old child, the teacher asked my restless, wiggling class, "How do you get close to God?"

The pat, easy answer was, "Read your Bible and pray."

None of us knew how to do those things very well. We just knew it was the right thing to say, and it was the most spiritually profound thing we could think of.

I will be the first one to say that reading your Bible and praying are vital to life, but I will also acknowledge that they are keys toward opening an incredible vault of treasures God has prepared for you . . . if you know how to use them. As a young woman, I found myself searching for a deeper walk with Christ that built upon the simple Sunday school formula. Writing a list of prayers and reading the Bible every day were easy, but my heart hungered for a more life-giving, revolutionary journey with Jesus. Envying the early disciples of the first century who walked with Jesus, I longed to follow him with their same connection and abandon.

> Faith became to me
> a programmed routine . . .
>
> An outward demonstration
> of Christianity
>
> That failed to
> engage my heart.

Simply put: there was more to the Christian life, and I wanted it—but I wasn't sure how to walk with Christ in a deep, fulfilling way.

Discovering Jesus, Discovering Discipleship

When I read the Gospels, I discovered a description of Jesus that defied my early Sunday school perceptions. A thoughtful

15

teacher and compelling communicator, he was a far cry from the pasty, stoically posed portraits my mind had painted of him. Instead, the Scriptures offer a fascinating glimpse of a hero who spoke truth, demonstrated love, and set the world on fire with his compelling message. In a time before social media or networking platforms, Jesus set an entire nation ablaze with his earth-shattering words—and he did it all in three and a half years. Christ's life was like lighting the fuse on a battery of fireworks: revolutionary principles exploding with riveting, world-changing beauty.

In the first century, many people didn't know what to do with Jesus. They either hated him, admired his boldness, marveled at his teachings—or loved his words and followed him. A master storyteller, Jesus packaged the vast principles of God's kingdom in simple metaphors the common person could understand. A grain of wheat, beautiful lilies in a field, a king throwing a wedding party, a lost son . . . his simple stories were mesmerizing, causing thousands to listen. The spiritual leaders of the day scowled and scoffed, afraid of his growing influence. This carpenter who healed the sick, turned water to wine for a wedding party, and knelt to wash the feet of his disciples was too much of an enigma to be ignored.

His band of disciples was also fascinating to discover. Like Robin Hood's Merry Men, each had a colorful background of various careers and talents, and they chose to follow Jesus and devote their lives to his cause. The term *disciple(s)* is used 273 times in the New Testament and simply means "learner" or "pupil." It is the most common word used to describe the men and women who followed Jesus as his personal students. Jesus led this tribe of followers through fields and thickets, in crowds of people and seasons of solitude, through times of fame, when the masses wanted to crown him king, and in times of persecution by jealous leaders. He offered moments of teaching and practical coaching to help them live from God's perspective.

Together
they lived and ate,
slept in chilly fields under the stars.

They ranged the deserts and hills,
followed by a multitude of
grateful,
curious,
skeptical crowds.

They witnessed his betrayal:
the mocking,
scourging
death blows of a hammer
tearing the flesh
of the Friend they loved.

Three days later,
in a blur
of tears and grief,
they stumbled into the garden of his burial
and saw
a vision of angels,
an empty tomb,
and there met the risen Lord.

Finally, the disciples realized with wide eyes that their Friend and Master was divine. He was "God with skin on," sent to bridge the gap between heaven and earth, opening divine access to a living relationship with the Father. Suddenly the term *disciple* took on a whole new meaning. They had not simply heard the teachings of an interesting rabbi—they had beheld the words of the God-man, sent to earth to show us how to live. Finally, when Jesus ascended to heaven, he spoke these words:

Go therefore and make disciples of all the nations, baptizing them in the name of the Father and of the Son and of the Holy Spirit.

Matthew 28:19

Now, *anyone can be a disciple*. That means me and you.

Blazing with life and purpose, this concept changes the whole idea of a life of faith. We are not meant to simply live inside a regimen of rules and call it spirituality. Jesus is alive, and he invites us to have the same deep connection with him that the disciples did on earth. In fact, the Scriptures clearly show how the early disciples continued their relationship with Jesus even after he ascended to heaven, because the Holy Spirit filled their hearts, connecting them all together in Christ. Now we too can walk closely with Jesus through each day—inviting the Spirit of God into our lives and following Christ's teachings. The Scriptures teach us that we too can answer his call, *Follow me*.

Becoming a Modern-Day Disciple

Since the word *disciple* means "learner," the term *disciplines* could be defined as "ways to learn." These ideas help us practice being a disciple of Jesus in our modern world. Far more than a list of rules or a textbook of prayers, they give us tools to practice discipleship in intentional ways, stirring our passion for Christ and helping us live it out. Like finding a trail of footprints left by Christ and his followers, we can set our feet on the same weathered path and discover *the Way* they walked.

> Spiritual disciplines
> help us break from our busy lives,
> shift our hearts toward heaven,
> give our souls space to breathe.
>
> They create space to partner
>   our hearts with God's.
> They unleash passion
>   to us,
>   in us,
>   through us.

Becoming a modern-day disciple means pausing long enough to listen . . . to hear the beat of Christ's heart . . . to learn what he loves . . . to match our footsteps to the rhythm of his. Spiritual practices unlock beautiful ways of living close to Christ.

Like the early disciples, some of us will be called to leave everything behind, while others will discover their calling begins on the front steps of their home. The apostles Peter, James, and John left prospering businesses, friends, and personal ambitions to be taught by this revolutionary Rabbi, while Martha, Mary, and Lazarus provided a safe place for the Master to stay while he traveled, and their kind hospitality was a beautiful gift of love to the Lord. Each discovered a marvelous adventure of following Jesus, offering their lives to him in varying ways.

My journey has taken a "leave everything behind" path, with a creative career that has opened tremendous opportunities around the world. Plus, my heart beats fast with the urge to spread the message of God's love in radical ways. That's the type of adventure God wove into in my heart. But other paths are no less effective— like that of my godmother, Julie, who works a nine-to-five job and lives out her faith in practical ways. When my mother was pregnant, Julie laid her gentle hands on her womb, praying that I would be a woman after God's heart . . . and she's never stopped praying. Spending hours on the phone with me to help me process emotions or decisions, offering advice, and simply carrying me in her prayerful heart have made her a pillar in my life. There's no way I can live a radical life of service without her. She is one of the heroes of the faith!

God's plan for your life is bigger than you can imagine . . . he has prepared some amazing divine adventures for you. If a few of the life lessons in my journey inspire you to move forward in yours, I will be thrilled. Let's move forward together as we walk with our Lord!

Embracing the Climb

Regardless of where your path takes you, spiritual practices lay the groundwork for God's plan, setting you up for success. As we build God's practical truths into our lives, we lay the necessary foundation for his unique plan to come to pass. Like strong layers of brick and mortar, these practices create a deep, sturdy platform to build on, regardless of what your personal structure looks like. The calling of God will be uniquely yours, but these basic principles challenge all of us to rise to the high calling of following Christ.

Perseverance Trail on the mountain in Alaska was a grueling commitment that resulted in a big payoff. Spiritual disciplines are often this way too. They take some hard work and intense focus, but they lead us to destinations just as beautiful as the refreshing mountain waterfall. They require an investment of time, self-awareness, and dedication to complete the journey. I can't promise that the path will be easy, but let me give you the same pep talk I gave my team:

"*You can do this.* The destination is worth the effort. Stay with me—you've got this! Let's do this together."

My prayer is that this book will offer a strategic road map for your journey. If you long to go deep in your relationship with God and walk out his will for your life, these pages will provide scriptural, time-tested methods to "get in shape" for your divine assignment. We'll explore core teachings of Jesus that show us how to become modern-day disciples. We'll journey around the world to discover ancient practices of the early church that offer fascinating, inspirational glimpses of how saints discovered and followed their adventure in Christ. We'll also discover how modern-day disciples are finding creative ways to live out their spirituality. Questions and activities at the end of each chapter will help personalize these truths for you so you can apply them to your own journey with Christ.

I'm excited to take this expedition with you! Your heart was made on purpose for a beautiful, intentional relationship with Jesus. Let's discover his grand adventure.

ONE

Say Yes

EMBRACING GOD'S GRACE

Soft light filled the wide, wood-beamed auditorium. The church was empty, warmed by laughter and music from hundreds of Sunday mornings—but now pin-drop quiet. I cautiously slipped inside, winding my way around the pews to where a shiny black grand piano stood. Folding back the lid and pressing the ivory keys, I sang with all my heart on the vacant stage. Somehow worshiping God from this place felt right. Still in high school, I had no idea of God's plan for my life, but the internal nudging of his call was still strong. It came alive during worship, even when playing to an empty hall.

Yet, the call felt far away too . . . like a gift labeled with my name, sitting just out of reach. The grid for living out God's adventure was strangely missing.

The call of God stirs deeply inside each of us: we desire a deeper connection with him and long to fulfill his plans for our lives, but sometimes we may feel like we're singing to an empty stage. Many times we long to do something beautiful, but the path is uncharted and overgrown with uncertainty. Some of us bury that call under the busyness of life, even using good things to stifle our awareness of it. Others try to fulfill their call with their own resources, believing they alone control their destiny. This gentle tugging from God has felt very real to my heart, but sometimes I've struggled with knowing how to take the next step of following him.

Through it all, God waits. He watches for those who will choose to partner with him rather than try to figure things out on their own.

> For the eyes of the LORD run to and fro throughout the whole earth, to show Himself strong on behalf of those whose heart is loyal to Him.
>
> 2 Chronicles 16:9

As we yield to Christ's plan, he releases a life of incredible purpose, bigger than anything we could dream up on our own. We realize that he plants our dreams as seeds within us, but they represent only a small part of what he has planned. Spiritual disciplines help us nurture that seed—just as a gardener invests water, light, fertilizer, and pruning into the growth process of a potential plant—until the fruit fills our lives and spills over into the world around us. Those who dare to follow Christ sign up for an incredible adventure!

God's plan for you is already in motion, and it was started long before you were born. He doesn't just give a nod in your direction—he is proactive, present, and persistently cheering for your best. His love is settled—you have it all. He's more invested in your life than you are because he's the one who made you. Really. It's true: *God is passionate about you.* Just sayin'!

Say Yes to Being Loved

God's pursuit of our hearts wasn't on my grid for success. It confused me. I thought I needed to impress him and win my way to heaven based on good behavior. I used to wince after doing something wrong, wondering if I could make it up to God somehow. Penance made more sense than grace.

Buried deep within us, human ambition and God's grace wrestle with each other on a daily basis, vying for our allegiance. The struggle is real: we are often prone to fighting for achievement rather than receiving the love he freely offers.

I feel it deeply . . . on the one hand, personal ambition offers the promise of success, but like a handful of snowflakes, it quickly melts away in my grasp.

You need to do better, try harder to please God, ambition says. *Success is just around the corner.*

This inner drive suggests a sense of goodness, pushing me to succeed by my wits in relationships, career, and faith. And I try. But as with the furious flapping of a moth drawn to a yellow flame, my wings are only singed the closer I get. The chase is maddening. And tiring.

On the other hand, God's grace offers the challenge to set my sights higher.

You are already loved, it whispers. *Stop trying to earn it. I already know the best plan for you. Just say yes to me.* I lean in close to listen, shutting out the familiar clamor of self-doubt and slowly tuning my soul toward the frequency of truth. *Your Father in heaven adores you—live from that place and be free!*

I breathe easier, knowing there is freedom, and strength, in this place. But it's not my norm. It doesn't come easily. It's a struggle, right? We have to learn how to be loved by God. And yield to his voice.

> We seek to be flawless.
> A dancer on a stage,
> commanding a standing ovation,
> smiling in the
> blushing glow
> of approval.

> But faith in Jesus
> works backward:
> we first receive the applause of heaven,
> which then inspires our dancing.

God's love and his plan were never meant to be two separate boxes: we receive his love, place our hand in his, and partner together in his grand adventure for our lives. But if we attempt to fulfill his plan without first receiving his love, we become a dancer auditioning for a part . . . hoping for approval . . . rather than knowing that we've already been chosen to take the stage with him. Grace whispers, *You are loved . . . come with me now. I'm ready . . . will you take my hand?*

It's Complicated

So many people approach God as an unsteady date. They think he's kind of interested in them, but they're not sure just *how much.* (*Should I call him or wait until he calls me?*) Believing he watches from a distance, they assume he's pretty busy with his job of running the universe and not too interested in a deeper connection. The conversation in our head could run like a scripted sequence of a complicated relationship.

I think he likes me, but I'm not sure if he actually wants to be involved in my life. I'm probably too messy for him . . . I'd probably ruin his reputation if we got serious. He might be "too holy" for me.

We feel safe with a distant relationship, knowing there's very little risk attached to that place. Perhaps we're afraid he might respond with a critical eye or judgmental stare if we move closer.

If we're honest, even some of us who have been Christians a long time spend much of our prayer life wrestling with questions like *God? Uh, are you listening? Are we okay? Are you mad at me today?*

We seek to be flawless.

A dancer on a stage,

commanding a standing ovation,

smiling in the

blushing glow

of approval.

But faith in Jesus

works backwards:

we first receive the applause of heaven,

which then inspires our dancing.

As Christians, we know in our heads that God loves us—even enough to give his life on the cross for us—but how many of us live from the place of his love? Do we experience it daily and recognize that he is consistently available to partner with us in the journey of life?

If this connection has potential, then maybe it's time for the next step. If you're like me, you've recognized there's more to a journey of faith than you've yet experienced, and you just need a little coaching on how to walk it out. We may feel safe when distancing ourselves from God, but in fact, the risk of not pursuing him is much greater. So let's move out of the "complicated" zone and learn a few tips for moving forward.

He Already Said Yes

Vividly, I recall speaking to a group of junior high kids at a wilderness retreat center. Packed into a chapel that was actually an old barn, a hundred bodies wiggled with boundless energy on the creaking benches. Each service ended by me asking them to write an honest prayer to God, fold it up, and bring it to the altar. When the mass of shuffling feet left the building, I returned to the altar, invading the sacred pile of prayers and peeking at a few notes so I could learn what was going on in the hearts of these kids. In scrawling, blotted script, I read, "I need help." Also, "I am confused—I don't know what to believe in. Help me find my way, please. And if you love me, please show me."

All week I threw my passion into sharing stories and Scriptures with the kids, sharing how much God wanted to be involved in their adventure. Racking my brain for the best testimonies, I challenged them to pray crazy prayers and dared them to believe God wanted to answer the desires of their hearts. As the week came to an end, I could see some hope rising in their little faces as they started to pray and seek God for themselves.

However, some of the kids had a view of God's grace that needed some tweaking. When chatting with them, I discovered they were making lists of requests for God to answer, hoping that his response would prove his presence in their lives. I winced, realizing that we can't negotiate with God's goodness in order to feel loved. Our encounters with Jesus are always based on what he's already done for us, and we simply get to respond to it.

From the dusty platform, I offered a new challenge.

"Some of you have been asking God to prove his love for you by doing something special," I said, gazing into hundreds of wide, young eyes. "I believe he will do this for you, but you need to know this truth: *Jesus already proved his love for you when he went to the cross.* You don't have to talk God into loving you, because he *died* for you. When he nailed your sin to the cross, he offered you a fresh start and the great adventure of walking with him: all you have to do is say yes."

The kids' eyes grew big as it dawned on them that they were begging for what already belonged to them: the Father's attention and love.

At the end of the final chapel service, I found myself engulfed in the arms of dozens of kids who surrounded me with hugs and high fives. After I was nearly knocked off my feet by a boy's walloping bear hug, a shy girl pressed a note into my hand. In pencil, she had sketched a picture of a cross under a sky of both sunshine and stars. The simple words read,

To: Rebecca
I AM LOVED

They got it, and they wanted me to know.

Whether you're in junior high or a little further along in your journey, one important step to adventuring with God is recognizing that he has already extended an invitation for the very thing we crave! He's not a distant God somewhere past the stars; he's present and real, and he deeply loves the humans he has made. Instead of wishing for, cajoling, or earning God's attention, we simply say yes to the great love he offers.

We love him, because he first loved us.

1 John 4:19 KJV

When you know you are loved, you simply get to say yes. You don't have to struggle for God's attention, because he is *longing* for a deeper walk with us. He doesn't have to consider it, and you're not too messy for him. He's already initiating, longing, waiting with anticipation for your heart to turn toward him, and he's not interested in just a "one-night stand" or fickle romance. He's ready for a long-term commitment, and he's willing to prove it.

When you pick up a book like this and choose to put the principles into practice, you're choosing to respond to his pursuit. We simply say yes to the One who desires intimacy far more than we do.

Say Yes to Spending Time with Him

In the beginning of creation, the world was perfect. The book of Genesis tells us that nature moved with a synergy and rhythm that required no destruction, and all the animals were herbivores, so no death was initiated in the cycle of life. God planted a garden with beautiful trees and a river as a home for the first man and woman. He gave them everything: food, beauty, work to do, and instructions to follow. They walked together, talked together, and thoroughly enjoyed each other's presence.

Then Adam and Eve said no. They disobeyed God's commandments when an evil serpent tricked them into eating fruit from a forbidden tree. Flushed with shame and suddenly aware of their nakedness, they awkwardly stitched together fig leaves as clothing to cover themselves. In the cool of the evening, their hearts sank at the last sound they wanted to hear . . . the voice of their beloved Maker and former companion called for them.

"Adam!" The Creator was coming to walk with the once-perfect delight of his creation. "Where are you?"

It was an epic scene: God came looking for his friend and found him hiding, terrified of the mess he had caused by disobeying the Creator's command. Innocence was lost, but God graciously made Adam and Eve clothes of animal skins, and the first death to enter the world was to cover human shame. It was only a temporary fix until the real sacrifice could be made, when the shame of humanity would be covered by the blood of the Lamb of God. As a willing victim for the crimes of humankind, Jesus endured the worst of humanity . . . fully God and fully man, he was betrayed, mocked, and cursed—absorbing the punishment of our sins and the broken relationship between humankind and God upon himself. In the middle of it all, Christ removed the distance between God and man. Christ's blood redeems sons and daughters back to the Father, who still calls, "My son, my daughter! Where are you? I'm seeking your presence . . . I long to walk with you in the cool of day and share life with you. Will you be my close companion?"

The obvious response ought to be, "Yes. I would love to spend time with you."

Adam and Eve, however, hid behind a self-constructed garment of excuses and blame-shifting. We are tempted to do the same, but our response can be different. With a simple prayer of repentance and forgiveness, our sin is covered and our relationship with God is restored. Because Christ has taken our shame and fully covered us with his robes of righteousness, we can gladly respond, "Lord, I'm here, and I want to walk with you!"

Saying Yes to God

Not only are we able to walk with God, but the Scriptures bring exciting news: *God loves to be pursued today*. He's not a stoic, expressionless companion—but rather, he longs to be intimately known and loved. For him, life is fresh, fascinating, and current. He sees potential in you today and wants to help you rediscover his grace over and over. Your love is valued and important to him. When speaking to the church in Ephesus, Jesus states,

> I know how many good things you are doing. I have watched your hard work and your patience; I know you don't tolerate sin among your members, and you have carefully examined the claims of those who say they are apostles but aren't. You have found out how they lie. You have patiently suffered for me without quitting.
>
> Yet there is one thing wrong; you don't love me as at first! Think about those times of your first love (how different now!) and turn back to me again and work as you did before; or else I will come and remove your candlestick from its place among the churches.
>
> Revelation 2:2–5 TLB

Jesus recounts all that this church was doing to please him, yet all of the good deeds and effort fell short because they had simply become routine. This church had begun to go through the motions of service, losing the heart-connection of intimacy with their God. They failed to take the journey with their first love—the soaring adventure of "How can I say *yes* to you?" Jesus's words blew on the low-but-glowing coals of their hearts with the reminder, *I see everything you DO for me, but I want your heart! Where is the blazing flame of spiritual hunger and love that you had in the start of our relationship? I've called you to a love life, and I miss you.*

As in any close relationship, there's more to it than a list of good things we *do* for each other. We say yes to spending time together. We say yes to activities that stoke the coals and rekindle the blaze.

Saying Yes with Purpose

My first attempts to grasp the grace of Christ were a bit awkward. Without a road map offering guidance to that destination, I made up a plan. The attributes of God I knew most about were his purity, holiness, and hatred of idolatry, so it made sense to craft a way to impress him based on those terms. Digging through closets and drawers, I made a pile of anything that looked "worldly" or "non-spiritual" and hauled garbage bags full of the castaway items to the trash. It was a brutal purging! Other times I would beg God to speak, standing in the pouring rain and telling him I wasn't going to budge until I heard from him. Desperately wanting to please and be close to him, I didn't have a clue about how to get there.

I was trying to be like the saints in history who slept on beds of nails or climbed mountains on their knees in an attempt to impress heaven. Instead of leaning on God's love, I made desperate plea bargains, trying to acquire his approval. I don't know if my personal purging or extreme behavior brought me any closer to God, but I believe God saw my heart. A few years later, some spiritual coaching helped redirect my focus into ways that really *did* bring a genuine connection to Christ. I was astonished to realize that some of the ways I was seeking to please him were so much different than what he actually wanted.

Today I'm still careful what items I keep in my house, because I want to honor God's standards of purity in my life. But I don't do massive purging or stand in the rain and pray simply to come up with a grand idea to win his attention. I am just glad God is patient with all of us. He sees the intentions of our hearts—not just our behavior. Those early steps demonstrated to God a willingness to follow Jesus when he *did* call me into many great adventures around the world. The truth is: *God loves our willingness!* Even our baby steps toward him are met with the beaming pleasure of our Father. Pursuing him, even with wobbly baby steps, brings him great joy.

Ways to Say Yes

Saying yes to biblically grounded guidance will release your soul to live free in the grace God has abundantly offered. It is far more practical than attempting to draw close to him in self-deprecating or demeaning ways. These principles stand as mile markers on the well-traveled road toward a thriving spiritual life. They are not legalistic formulas or rules for success. Accept the truth that God's love and grace surround you every day, and you will be connected to the heart of God. You will be motivated to invest in your relationship with him. The more you lean into his grace, the more prepared you will be for your calling and the great adventure Jesus has destined for your life.

God's Word provides some great ways to say yes to his open invitation of a deeper relationship with him. When we're feeling overwhelmed and tired, Jesus invites us to come to him and rest:

> Come to Me, all you who labor and are heavy laden, and I will give you rest.
>
> Matthew 11:28

When we are filled with worry and fear, God invites us to say yes to him by praying over all our needs and receiving his peace:

> Be anxious for nothing, but in everything by prayer and supplication, with thanksgiving, let your requests be made known to God; and the peace of God, which surpasses all understanding, will guard your hearts and minds through Christ Jesus.
>
> Philippians 4:6–7

When faced with detours and delays in life, God invites us to say yes by waiting on him, and he promises fresh strength for our journey:

> But those who wait on the LORD
> Shall renew their strength;
> They shall mount up with wings like eagles,
> They shall run and not be weary,
> They shall walk and not faint.
>
> Isaiah 40:31

Saying yes to God means choosing to partner with the One who loves to come alongside our journey and has a beautiful adventure planned for our lives.

Your Turn

- Describe a time when you have said yes to God in your journey.
- How does the tension between personal ambition and God's grace play a part in your life?
- How does God's grace help us pursue him?
- What are some ways you can say yes to God today?

Spiritual Practice

Take communion as an act of worship, recognizing that Christ's love cannot be earned but has already been extended to you. Jesus gave his life for you! He has initiated the relationship—all we need to do now is say *yes* to his love. As you take the bread and grape juice, recognize that you are receiving the perfect love that is freely given to you. Read Luke 22:17–20, and say a prayer of your own or use the words below:

Jesus, thank you for extending your love to me on the cross. By taking these elements, the bread reminds me how your body was brutally broken, and the grape juice recalls the blood you shed for my sin. I choose to receive them as a token of your desire for relationship and say yes to your love.

TWO

The Quiet Place

MAKING SPACE FOR PRAYER

The day had been full of Celtic experiences: bagpipes, kilts, and energetic Highland games. A whirlwind of filming and interviews, it had been an exhilarating day on location in Scotland. My head was spinning, my mind still running off the momentum of the day. Now, back at my lodging at a large mission house, I unpacked my cameras and took a deep breath . . . letting a swirl of thoughts settle and listening to the thud of my own heart.

Pray . . . I need to pray. I need to slip away and connect with my Savior.

In the muted shadows, while the household and other guests were sleeping, I slipped down the wide hallway of the old stone building and into a small music room that was open to visitors. Flipping on the light, I sighed with relief. Inside, several guitars waited for anyone inclined to play. The small room became my personal cathedral. I picked an instrument and sat cross-legged on the floor, softly strumming the nickel strings and focusing my attention on the Lord in worship.

Immediately I sensed the presence of Christ, like a friend who had been waiting for me to arrive, as he reached out to meet my heart. He knew each moment of the day and desired to talk about it. Unloading my dreams at the feet of Jesus, I told him of my passion to create a film that would touch hearts and impact lives. I prayed for my team, thanking God for their hard work and praying for a restful, rejuvenating night of sleep for them. In the solace of that late-night conversation, the wheels of my racing brain slowed as I realized that God was deeply interested and involved in my story. He connected with me. I connected with him. As I made time for the quiet place of prayer, I focused on the purpose of glorifying God, and peace reigned.

Life hadn't stopped . . . I had. Even during a crazy season of movement and managing the unpredictable moments of life, the door was still open to the quiet place of prayer. In fact, it was just a hallway away.

> In the quiet place
> Christ stills us
> Centers us
> Shapes us
> Like a potter's hands
> on a wobbly lump of clay.
>
> Caring about our journey.
> Knowing our struggles.
> Meeting us where we are.
> Every time.

If we're honest, we'll probably admit that making time for God is easier said than done. Our world offers so many opportunities for entertainment, education, and family, yet nothing can replace the beauty of making time for the quiet place of prayer. Yet, if we study the spiritual disciplines of the early church, we'll discover that they had creative, intentional ways of building prayer into their lives. They had busy lives too—can you imagine living during a time without modern conveniences like cars, washing machines, running water, and supermarkets? Even though their time revolved around hard work and basic survival skills, they still found clever ways to pray. Entire communities were affected and even saved as a result of their lives of prayer.

One of these places that offer a bounty of tips for our journey into the quiet place of prayer is an ancient British isle called Holy Island. Come with me—let's travel to this ancient soil where the quiet place of prayer was practiced for hundreds of years. Together, we'll discover beauty, inspiration, and practical tips from believers who found help and peace in their quiet times with God . . .

Holy Island—a Rhythm of Prayer

Gentle waves tossed against a pebbled beach. Misty air filled the lungs of pilgrims with the crisp scent of salt and sea. The silence was punctuated by the lonesome cry of gulls searching for mussels where the tide had uncovered thousands of purple shells. Across the sea, the mainland was still visible, offering a distant glimpse of the modern, bustling world to an island that was, in many ways, content to exist without it.

Following the long strides of my island guide and host, I shouldered my backpack of cameras and tromped the green turf on the Holy Island of Lindisfarne. When our path abruptly led us down the face of a jagged cliff, a little thrill of wonder went up my spine. I braced my tripods against rocks, safely out of the wind that whipped over the Northumberland coast, and set up my film gear for a scenic film shoot on the rocky ledge. There was just enough earthy room to set up my cameras while my guest settled onto a stone outcrop that overlooked miles of ocean and a few distant islands.

The shoot location of Lindisfarne is accessible from the mainland for about seven hours at a time, then for the next four or five hours it's cut off by the tide, which completely covers the single road connecting the island to the mainland. Apart from being a novelty for tourists, Holy Island is known for its fascinating past: fifteen hundred years ago, this island was solely inhabited by Christian monks and scholars who formed a community known for prayer.

My guest for this interview was island resident, author, and well-traveled speaker Andy Raine, who knew every inch of cliffs and turf on Holy Island after living there over thirty years. Well-versed in Celtic history, he pulled from his vast knowledge of early Christianity to unpack fascinating tales of early believers who intentionally cultivated a life of prayer on this island.

Cameras rolling, I listened to his melodic British accent tell stories of ancient prayer from the island's history.

"We tend to think of hermits as people who just want to get away from the world, or are perhaps a bit antisocial," Andy began with a chuckle. "But that wasn't the understanding in the Celtic times: they saw the hermit as the person called to the front lines, brave enough and humble enough to face the enemy forces away from distractions, so that they could pray in a more wholehearted way."

Standing on the cliffs overlooking the sea, it was easy to imagine early Christians pushing off in a small coracle boat toward the wild blue-and-gray islands where no distractions could keep them from their time with God. Their community would have been self-sustaining, fishing the sea and farming the land in addition to copying the Scriptures and spending time in prayer. With no electronics or modern conveniences, all the work was done by hand or with crude tools. Yet even during their busy schedule, they intentionally made space in their life for God, and the result often impacted their nation in amazing ways.

From Andy, I learned the beautiful story of Aidan, who founded this community around AD 635. It goes like this:

> One spring during Lent, Aidan pushed off from Holy Island in his little boat for further solitude on a nearby island. He gazed across

the waters to Bamburgh Castle on the mainland and saw that an enemy army led by King Penda had attacked the grounds. Piling bundles of sticks against the castle walls, Penda's men hoped to smoke out the inhabitants inside. Being too far away to offer any physical assistance, Aidan fell on his knees and prayed, "Lord, see what evil Penda does!"

Immediately, a wind rose from the sea, blowing the smoke away from the castle and saving the lives of the terrified countrymen inside. The nation was saved, all because of the prayers of one man on an island who had captured the attention of God.

"I love the relationship between Aidan and God," Andy commented. "He's able to say, 'Lord, do you see that?' There's an immediacy with God where he's able to name evil and have Justice respond."

In this quiet place, the saints talked to God. God listened. He talked to them. They listened. The rhythm of prayer was both simple and profound. From that intentional choice to make time for God, many lives were saved.

Making Space

We might not all have a wild island in our backyard or a coracle we can hop into so we can paddle away for a few weeks of seclusion, but the core principle remains the same: one of the greatest keys to drawing close to God is cultivating quality time with him. Creating this quiet space requires thought and planning, and it usually doesn't come naturally. With busy lives and families, there is always a "good cause" calling for our attention. But the rewards are much more far-reaching than we can imagine.

Christ led by example in this area. Jesus had a busy life! He wasn't isolated—rather, he was deeply invested in the lives of people and helping them. Yet we often see him stepping away from the crowds and even his own friends to get alone with the Father, and he helped his disciples do the same thing. During pivotal points

In this quiet place,

the saints talked to God.

God listened. He talked

to them. They listened.

The rhythm of prayer was

both simple and profound.

in his ministry, we're told Jesus went into "desert places" to pray, far away from distractions and the bustle of his hectic schedule. Here are a few examples:

- Before selecting twelve apostles, Jesus climbed a mountain and spent the night alone in prayer. In the quiet of those evening hours, he prepared for this massive decision that would affect the rest of his ministry.

Now it came to pass in those days that He went out to the mountain to pray, and continued all night in prayer to God. And when it was day, He called His disciples to Himself; and from them He chose twelve whom He also named apostles.

Luke 6:12–13

- Even when crowds with thousands of people were demanding his time, Jesus found a way to graciously meet the need and also stay intentional about his time of prayer. Another time, during a season of grief after hearing the news that his cousin John the Baptist had been killed, he called his disciples away for some alone time in the desert. Unfortunately, the crowds were so intent on being close to him that they crashed his private prayer meeting.

When Jesus heard it, He departed from there by boat to a deserted place by Himself. But when the multitudes heard it, they followed Him on foot from the cities.

Matthew 14:13

Jesus was moved with compassion and decided to meet the needs of the people, even multiplying five loaves and two fish to give them a meal, but then he sent his disciples away and retreated into the wilderness to pray. Even during the busyness of the season, he found a way to set boundaries and make time with his Father.

And when He had sent the multitudes away, He went up on the mountain by Himself to pray. Now when evening came, He was alone there.

Matthew 14:23

- In the garden of Gethsemane, Jesus spent the last hours before his betrayal in prayer. He brought several of his closest friends with him, then he stepped a little farther into the olive grove and poured his heart out to his Father, knowing that strength for this difficult moment could come only from God.

Then Jesus came with them to a place called Gethsemane, and said to the disciples, "Sit here while I go and pray over there." And He took with Him Peter and the two sons of Zebedee, and He began to be sorrowful and deeply distressed. Then He said to them, "My soul is exceedingly sorrowful, even to death. Stay here and watch with Me."

He went a little farther and fell on His face, and prayed, saying, "O My Father, if it is possible, let this cup pass from Me; nevertheless, not as I will, but as You will."

Matthew 26:36–39

In each intense situation, we see Jesus stepping away from the energy of the group and slipping away for some private time in prayer. This isn't to say that community wasn't important to him, but Christ's strength, stamina, and courage didn't come from crowds of awestruck people or even time spent with his friends but rather from his times of prayer. These conversations with his Father were not some kind of penance or afterthought, but passionate discussions that were deliberately woven into the very thread of his life and during his most important decisions. During times of grief, intense ministry, and despair, he always made time to pray.

Practicing the Quiet Place

Practicing the quiet place of prayer in our modern world is based on the same principles we see in the life of Jesus. The first step is very simple yet often hard to practice: *step away*. Mute the phone, take a walk, plan a retreat, or do something that takes you away from the noise of ordinary life. Maybe you start with fifteen minutes a day, an hour a week, or two days a month. The idea is to make a space in your schedule that's set aside for God, the Creator of the universe, who is ready to meet with you. As you do, you'll discover the incredible value and beauty of spending time with God.

As in any relationship, embrace the adventure of sharing your heart with God. When you step into the quiet space, don't feel like you have to brace yourself for boredom or stare at the ceiling. This is a time to communicate the needs of your heart to the Father who loves to be involved in your life. What are your concerns, ideas, and moments you are thankful for? Tell them to God and invite his input. Everyone is different, so don't feel like your prayer time has to look like anyone else's. The goal is to give God your undivided attention and connect with him in the way that works for you. Here are some ideas:

- **Partner with praise:** Opening with praise and thanksgiving is a great way to start prayer time. Reflecting on the goodness of God and how great he is shifts our focus off of our needs and onto him. Reading a psalm out loud is a great opener. (See Pss. 23, 27, 100, 117.)

- **Journal your prayers:** One of the greatest ways to connect with God is through prayer journaling. Write down whatever is going on in your life, being honest with your struggles and the things you'd like to see changed. Include inner battles as well as prayer requests for people. The biggest key is to write from your heart, and don't be afraid to express the emotions, challenges, and joys you're facing. After you've written everything down, open your Bible and start to read. You'll be amazed to find how often the verses you see speak to what you've written!

- **Pray for others:** Is there anyone with a need that comes to mind? Bring them to the Lord in prayer. Be specific: Where is there a need? Protection, provision, open doors, deliverance from fear, and health issues are all great things to pray for as we lift up others. As you pray, ask the Lord to reveal his heart for the person or situation so that you can pray for what he desires too.

- **Listen and speak:** Focus on both listening and speaking during this time, both of which take place in a good relationship. Express your heart, make your requests, verbalize your thanks, and also take time to listen for the Father's response. You may feel drawn to read certain passages of Scripture, or you may have a routine of Bible reading that you follow. Sometimes the Holy Spirit may prompt you to pray over or ponder a specific area in your life and seek his wisdom and perspective. Prayer is an interactive conversation.

- **Be honest:** Some of my best prayer times are simply moments when I talk about my worries, my needs, and the desires of my heart with God. Prayer is a safe place with the Father who deeply loves you, so don't feel like you need to be perfect or make your world clean and pretty for him. He knows it all anyway, so why not be honest about the areas you're struggling with and invite him in?

- **Go outdoors:** Jesus often climbed mountains to pray, using the quiet of nature as a way to connect with his Father. If you love nature, block out some time to hike a trail, sit on a park bench, or take your shoes off and sink your toes into a cool stream. Bring the joy of nature into your time of prayer.

- **Positional prayer:** It may feel archaic, but there are times when getting on your knees in prayer or moving in a way to express worship are great exercises. Scripture tells us that Moses fell on his face and Daniel knelt in prayer, and the Psalms even call us to "praise his name in the dance" (Ps. 149:3 KJV). Don't limit yourself to sitting in a chair while you pray—get creative!

Your personal prayer time is all about you and God having a conversation, so feel free to explore what means of communication works best for you. Maybe your grandmother sat in her rocking chair singing hymns as she talked to Jesus, but you may feel more comfortable packing a picnic lunch and hiking a scenic trail for your quiet time. Experiment and look for ways you can develop your prayer life and make it your own.

Live Your Prayers, Pray Your Life

Practicing the quiet place of prayer is powerful, because it's our special time with Jesus. Yet, it doesn't have to end when "normal life" resumes. The spiritual practice of prayer can extend beyond our moments of solitude and become a part of the rhythm of our day.

Recently I reconnected with my friends on Holy Island. From the warmth of my living room, I placed an international call to Andy Raine and asked him to expound the history he'd shared on the cliffs. Ninety minutes and seven pages of notes later, I was still jotting notes about how these early saints spent time with God.

Unfolding the universal power of prayer, Andy took me back to the era of history in England when the Bible was not available for everyone like it is today. A thousand years before Wycliffe translated the Bible into the language of the common people, only the monks and bishops could read the Latin, Greek, and Hebrew writings that comprise God's Word. Nor would it have mattered if the Bible had been translated into a common tongue: in the Dark Ages, commoners couldn't read at all. For the working man, reading the Scriptures was an unattainable goal.

But they could still pray. The monks taught the common people ways to connect with God as they farmed and fished throughout the day. In this way, they wove prayer into their everyday lives.

"Faith was not something separated from life, but was absolutely integrated," Andy said, revealing how prayer wove itself into the daily lives of believers. "We have records of prayers for milking cows, prayers for laying a fire or going on a journey, prayers for putting your clothes on in the morning, and at the same time, you'd put on Christ. Life, prayer, and faith were intimately connected and not put into separate compartments.

"In this way, *they could live their prayers and pray their lives.*"

I was struck by the phrase, turning it around in my mind like a shiny new coin. What could it look like to "pray your life"? For these early believers, daily prayers could be as simple as asking God to bless their cow, which offered daily milk, or requesting protection for their fishing boat in the middle of a stormy sea. In this way, they were inviting God into their world in ways that reminded them of his constant presence.

We too can "pray our lives" by extending the place of prayer into our ordinary day as they did. By praying to God throughout our day, we're bringing our quiet place with him into our day-to-day life. Our prayer life expands. So does the peace, because we're inviting the One who loves us deeply into our world. Life becomes an adventure we share with Christ, knowing he desires to be lovingly invested in our story. In your story! Your prayers are conversations with the One who loves you more than anyone else does, and he loves to "do life" with the ones he loves. The quiet place doesn't have to end when your quiet time is over. As you continue your prayers to God within your day, his presence and peace expand to the rest of your life.

To pray our lives looks completely different for each person, because no two lives are the same. Creating ways to engage with God during the day is a great goal, and there are so many fun ways to make it happen. Here are a few ideas:

- Play worship music around the house during the day.
- If you have kids, play songs that have lyrics of Scripture verses. The kids will learn the verses and you will too.
- Write Scriptures or inspirational sayings on note cards and place them on your mirror as reminders of God's love.
- Walk through your home and ask God to bless each room.
- Prayer-walk your neighborhood, asking God to protect the homes and draw each person to himself.
- Start a prayer box for your family: Have each person write a prayer request weekly and add it to the box. At the end of the year, read through the requests and praise God for his answers.
- Find a prayer partner and meet once a week to talk and pray.

Adventures in Prayer

As we cultivate this spiritual practice, we form a lifestyle of prayer. By starting with a regular quiet time, we offer God an intentional time to connect and focus on him. When we bring prayer into our day, learning to pray our lives, we discover that prayer becomes woven into our daily rhythm of life.

There were also times when the early saints offered God their lives of prayer in a very unique way: they made themselves available to God, ready for his prompting to pray when he saw fit. It's said they would "take themselves to prayer" for reasons beyond personal retreat or refreshment. During these times, the early saints would *make themselves available to God*. They were not entering

Your prayers are
conversations with
the One who loves you
more than anyone else does,
and he loves to "do life"
with the ones he loves.

into prayer for their own lists of wants or needs, or to get away from the frustrations of life, but rather to be "on call" if needed. Perhaps there was a person, town, or even political situation that required prayer—these men and women had prepared themselves to pray for whatever the situation required as the Spirit of God impressed it on their hearts. Sometimes they were involved in spiritual warfare, while other times they simply saw time alone with God as a season to just enjoy him, and they considered the extended time in prayer a "honeymoon" with their Beloved. It is said the local townspeople always felt grateful when this type of saint lived nearby because they knew they were being prayed for, and it made them feel safe.

Being available to God in this way requires self-sacrifice, humility, and a deep level of trust that God cares enough to actually clue me in on what is on his heart. It may be that throughout my day I sense his call to prayer for a particular person or situation. Or perhaps I may need to step away during the day and find a quiet place . . . not because I've routinely scheduled it, but because I'm sensing the call to listen to him. The beautiful thing about God is that he often weaves prayer prompts into things that I am already concerned about . . . perhaps a cue to pray over a family member, a situation at my job, or a friend I haven't thought of in a long time. He loves prompting our hearts to notice what he sees, and then he calls us to partner with him in prayer to see results.

The Scriptures are packed with stories of prayer warriors who chose extended times in wilderness places to be available to God. Their prayer lives were always routine . . . sometimes they were prompted to spend extended seasons in solitude because they were called by God to pray. Moses spent forty days on a mountain praying for his nation, Daniel fasted for three weeks and was visited by an angel, and Elijah heard the still, small voice of God in a cave. Their time was rewarded when God moved as a result of their intercession. Nations have been changed because of people who made themselves available to God in prayer.

Although we may never be called to a lifestyle of intense solitude, it can be a great practice to say, "Lord, I make myself available to you in prayer. Will you prompt me to pray today?"

In this way, prayer becomes a constant open conversation between you and God. Maybe you will have the fleeting thought to pray for a person, a situation, or even a nation that wouldn't have normally come to mind, or perhaps you will just be led to enjoy the presence of God and worship.

These practices help us find the well-worn paths of prayer that led the authors of Scripture to write,

Pray without ceasing.

1 Thessalonians 5:17

We may start with an intentional quiet time of prayer, whether it be fifteen minutes or an hour a day. Then we learn to "pray our lives" by bringing prayer into our world. Even further, we become available to God by asking him to prompt us to prayer, inviting him into our world and availing ourselves to his service. Building our rhythm of prayer can be as unique as we are!

Worthwhile Prayers

God loves giving us his undivided attention. When we step into the quiet place of prayer, we give him ours. As a result, our faith grows and our hearts thrive when spending personal time with the Creator of the universe.

> The Lord listens.
> He waits for you to speak.
> Because your voice matters to him.
>
> You listen.
> Tuning your ear to his voice.
> Because his voice matters to you.

Cultivating the quiet place of prayer is one of the most powerful spiritual practices in Christianity. It doesn't matter where you are in your faith journey; talking to God and listening for his response is a beautiful way to take action and invest in your relationship with him. The journey will take you in the steps of men and women of faith who have weathered this ancient trail for thousands of years. Yet it's a path that's just for you, too, because God has invited *you* to explore this place of prayer. And when you do, you'll discover this divine adventure is yours to enjoy.

Your Turn

- When you think about making time for prayer, what are the first thoughts that come to mind?
- Does the idea intrigue you or fill you with apprehension? Explain.
- What are some ways that you can best connect with God (journaling, walking, etc.)?
- What's a good plan to start implementing this into your life in a greater way?

Spiritual Practice

Plan a special time for you and Jesus; consider it a date. Block some time out of your schedule for a few hours and go somewhere that's quiet. Bring whatever best helps you enter into prayer: worship music, your Bible, a journal, etc. If you feel like you could be bored, make a plan beforehand of what you'd like to accomplish. Bring a canvas and paints, a guitar, or a prayer list of special needs from friends and family members. Make this sacred space a time between you and God, sharing your heart and listening for his.

THREE

Search the Scriptures

UNPACKING GOD'S LOVE LETTER

Recently a friend gave me a three-hundred-year-old Bible. Her husband, a book collector, had stumbled upon this old copy of the Scriptures that looked like a relic in a period film . . . the leather cover, worn and weathered with age beneath intricate metal clasps, wrapped around yellowed pages and carefully penned German calligraphy text. The sheer age of this book was daunting . . . its letters were mysterious and strange. As much as I would have liked to read its worn pages, all I could do was admire the finely inscribed text and imagine what it meant.

Today we can pick up a Bible in our language with various translations, cover options, and commentary themes. We don't have to squint at tiny text or translate it into another language in order to read it. Yet, just as the old Germanic text was impossible for me to decipher, many people in our generation have labeled the Bible as an outdated book that is too hard to understand or apply in today's world. The words may feel controversial, with complicated themes that may be easily misunderstood. We admire the historicity of the book but are mystified by the content. Some readers simply favor placing the Scriptures on a shelf rather than learning to unpack the words to discover the beauty and truth for themselves. And yet, there is so much to be discovered when we do.

> We often avoid the Scriptures
> because we haven't fallen in love with them.
>
> And yes,
> it is possible to fall in love
> with this amazing book.

Truth be told, the Bible is an incredible manuscript that is worthy of our time and attention and represents the core of true love and authentic truth of the Christian faith. Not only does it hold timeless revelation about God, his plan for the world, and his heart for you, but it also comes alive as the Holy Spirit brings verses that leap off the page and help us hear his voice in our lives.

Not only will you find truth for yourself but you'll discover incredible tools to love others well, all penned by the One who gave his life for us. These results don't happen by osmosis—you can't put a Bible under your pillow and wake up the next day infused with a passion for Scripture—but if you understand the tools presented in this chapter, you'll discover just how simple it is to connect with God through his Word. The Bible is God's love letter to humanity, and when you have the skills to start digging, you'll discover why this book is the ultimate bestseller.

Getting Wet

When living in San Diego, I enjoyed sinking my toes into the warm sand while watching surfers ride the waves in the ocean. Paddling into the blue water, they waited for the perfect wave to swell, jumped on their boards, and let the foamy surf carry them to shore. I imagined how much fun it would be to surf those waves, but I had a problem: I didn't want to leave the beach! Undertows . . . riptides . . . wipeouts . . . they sounded pretty scary. The whole thing felt confusing, so I made myself a little nest of warm sand and decided to stay on the beach.

Many people treat God's Word the same way I did surfing. They like the idea of hearing from God, but they are wary of diving into God's Word for themselves. Getting into the Scriptures can be risky . . . it might require more of a learning curve than we're comfortable with, and some of the verses can be confusing. We like the thought of having the Scriptures come alive to us, but what if we spend time waiting for the "wave" that never comes? Heaven forbid we would actually be *bored*!

It would be nice if we could just open the Bible, point to a passage, and BAM! the Scriptures leap off the page each time. But the general principle is this: God's Word comes alive for people who have become students of the Word. The truth is, we won't actually have amazing experiences with God's Word until we do more than sunbathe on the beach: it's time to put on a wet suit and be willing to dive in. So let's start by learning some simple ways to delve into God's Word.

Ancient Truth

The Bible is a deeply engaging book. It's not a quick read or a three-step manual for a happier life. The rich layers are much like a movie with such a profound story line that you see a fresh twist or undertone each time you experience it. Our journey to unpacking its pages starts by exploring what makes this book so unique and worthy of our attention.

When thinking about digging into God's Word, we're talking about studying one of the oldest recorded books in history, handwritten and passed down through the ages by saints and scholars, and now placed in our hands for personal reflection and wisdom.

God's Word comes
alive for people who
have become students
of the Word.

With over five billion copies sold,[1] this book has impacted more lives than any other written work, yet it never grows old or goes out of print because the timeless truths continue to touch all ages, races, cultures, and social classes.

> It is the most influential book
> ever written.
>
> Penned by God
> for his children.

Let's look at a few facts that outline just how amazing this book is.

United themes: The Scriptures were written in three languages: Hebrew, Greek, and Aramaic, by forty authors on three continents (Asia, Africa, and Europe), during a period of fifteen hundred years, yet there is a unity and cohesiveness within the themes of the writers.

Historical accuracy: Unlike other religious writings, the Bible is completely backed by archaeology and geography. If you visit the Middle East, you'll see a landscape marked with artifacts thousands of years old that verify the authenticity of cities and regions named in the accounts. Other writings, such as the Book of Mormon, have fictionalized lists of geographical places, which make them harder to trust. For a nonfiction book, the Bible is spot-on with locations that span thousands of years.

Reliability: More than any other written work, the New Testament has been preserved in more than 5,800 Greek manuscripts.[2] (The runner-up is Homer's *Iliad* at 2,000.[3]) From a scholar's perspective, this proves it to be a reliable text, and what you see today is in fact what was actually written in the first century by the first disciples of Jesus.

Eyewitnesses: The majority of the Gospels were written by first-person sources and those living at the time of Christ, and every major point of the birth, death, and resurrection of Christ is confirmed by all the authors. Many of the authors became martyrs for this faith, which also gives credit to their writings: not many authors are willing to die for their work.

Prophecies: It would be impossible for a group of people to have written this book, because it takes a power outside of time and space to make it cohesive. Before the birth of Christ, God gave his prophets signs and details about his life. Consider a few of the specific prophecies given about the promised King in the Old Testament, many made over seven hundred years before the birth of Christ, which were fulfilled in his life:

- **He would be born of a virgin** (foretold: Isa. 7:14; fulfilled: Matt. 1:21–23).
- **The King would be from the lineage of the tribe of Judah and the line of David** (foretold: Isa. 9:6–7; fulfilled: Luke 1:32–33).
- **He would go to Egypt and live in Nazareth** (foretold: Hosea 11:1; fulfilled: Matt. 2:14–15).
- **Galilee would receive light** (foretold: Isa. 9:1–2; fulfilled: Matt. 4:13–16).
- **The King would ride a donkey into Jerusalem** (foretold: Zech. 9:9; fulfilled: Matt. 21:1–7).
- **He would be betrayed** (foretold: Ps. 41:9; fulfilled: Luke 22:47–48).
- **As a captive, he would be sold for thirty pieces of silver** (foretold: Zech. 11:12–13; fulfilled: Matt. 26:14–16).
- **The King would be mocked and given vinegar to drink** (foretold: Ps. 69:21; fulfilled: John 19:28–30).
- **His hands and feet would be pierced** (foretold: Ps. 22:16, Zech. 12:10; fulfilled: John 20:25–27).[4]
- **Soldiers would gamble for his garments** (foretold: Ps. 22:18; fulfilled: Matt. 27:35–36).

- **In death, he was destined to be buried with the rich** (foretold: Isa. 53:9; fulfilled: Matt. 27:57–60).
- **Immortal, he would be raised from the dead** (foretold: Pss. 16:10, 49:15; fulfilled: Matt. 28:2–7, Acts 2:22–32).

These are just a few of the specific prophecies about Jesus that were predicted in writing *hundreds of years before his birth*! No other religious leader, such as Mohammad (Islam), Joseph Smith (Mormonism), or Charles Taze Russell (Jehovah's Witnesses), can make such a claim. Only God could have masterminded this feat in writing and scripted a book that so accurately portrays the coming of Jesus in this specific way.

Broad content: If a caring God wrote a book on the topics that most affect our lives, we'd expect it to cover subjects that matter most to our physical, emotional, moral, spiritual, and social well-being, just to name a few. Some topics could include

- morality
- government
- family
- sex
- health
- emotional awareness
- art
- finances
- what God expects from us
- how the earth began and how it will end
- how to treat other humans

In the Bible, we discover all this and more. Not only does it cover all of these topics, but with a proper understanding of the teachings, the perspective is just as relevant today as it was two thousand years ago. It covers all of these broad topics with amazing detail so that we can continue to unpack them today.

Making It Real

As a teenager, I learned many of the interesting facts about the Bible from my parents. I came to the conclusion that the Bible is an amazing book, yet I'll be honest: I had no idea how to unpack it for myself. I had a factual understanding of the Bible, but I wasn't interested in reading more than a few verses a day—much less creating a spiritual discipline of delving into God's Word on a regular basis—because I had no heart-connection with the words. The Bible was a distant truth but not a life-giving source.

One reason for this was that I had only connected with the *written* Word, but I hadn't yet encountered the *living* Word of God. The Scriptures state that God's Word is alive . . . not just a stagnant book with a lot of old writings. The words within this book bring clarity to tough situations, hope in discouragement, wisdom in tough times, and discernment when truth feels unclear. When the words come alive to our hearts, it's a sword we can wield in battle.

> For the word of God is living and powerful,
> and sharper than any two-edged sword,
> piercing even to the division of soul and spirit,
> and of joints and marrow,
> and is a discerner of the thoughts and intents of the heart.
> Hebrews 4:12

When God's Word comes alive to us, the book becomes more than a list of historical facts and figures. We discover it's a powerful compass to chart our own personal adventure, filled with wisdom and application that speak to every area of our lives. As we read and ponder the significance of the words, the Author himself comes close, applying his script to our story.

Jigsaw Puzzle

I started falling in love with the Scriptures in a curious way. I was a teenager living in a small town, when a minister from the city came to our local Bible study and started teaching the Scriptures with passion. His notes on the white board were often smudged simply because he got so excited while writing that his hands had a hard time keeping up with his thoughts. He taught us to "let Scripture interpret Scripture" and how to find multiple verses on the same topic to get a big picture on what the Bible was saying. His energy was compelling, and I knew he had something I didn't have . . . a true excitement about the Bible.

I went home and found the only study tool I knew how to use, a copy of *Strong's Concordance*. It had over a thousand pages of tiny print that listed every Hebrew and Greek word in the Bible translated into English and showed every time in Scripture a specific word was used.

After lugging the massive book to my bedroom, I thought of a topic I wanted to know more about. The more I researched, the more I became fascinated by what I discovered.

> Like a jigsaw puzzle
> the verses are pieces
> of a much bigger picture.
>
> Like a treasure hunt
> each Scripture is a clue
> pointing to the prize.

At the end of my study, I was astonished to realize that four hours had passed and I had not been bored for a single moment.

This led to more studies. Soon I started to share what I was learning with groups of young people. Many times there were tears and open hearts, and I began to watch God's Word have an amazing effect on people to heal and transform lives. The beautiful thing about the Scriptures is that the Author is very present and loves to use his words to set people free. The more we learn how to study his message, the more we are truly able to help others understand his love and truth.

So let's talk about some practical ways we can delve into God's Word. By learning some simple skills, you'll be off the sand and surfing the waves in no time.

Tools for Unpacking

Even though the Bible has been printed more than any other book in history, it requires more than just reading; to get the most out of it, we have to unpack the beautiful layers of inspiration and connect with the heart of the Author. While anyone can pick up the stories and read them, there are additional ways we can think about the words and let them sink into our hearts. Here are a few tools that can help us go deeper.

Reading a Devotional

If you have a difficult time understanding what the Scriptures are saying, invest in a good Christian devotional. Find a topic you are interested in, read it daily, and journal your response. Ask yourself questions like these:

- What's the takeaway, or what's the writer's main point?
- What can I apply to my own life?

Verbalize or write a prayer, asking God to write his Word in your heart and help you live it out.

Bible Journaling

For creatives, consider purchasing an adult Bible coloring book that offers Scripture and allows you to color in the designs as you meditate on God's Word. Put on some worship music, pull out your colored pencils, and think about the verse while adding your creative spin to the pages. Some books even have a daily devotional and a coloring page so you can get into God's Word and then get creative in the same day. Physiologists know that if you connect the left side of your brain (logistic) with the right side of your brain (artistic), you'll be more apt to retain the knowledge, so this helps with absorbing God's Word too.

Using a Concordance

Thankfully, you won't have to flip through a massive concordance like I did, because we can access the same information with a flick of a finger on an app. My favorite is e-Sword on my iPhone (or MySword for Android), which contains the entire *Strong's Concordance*. It has no commentaries, just Scripture. When you type in a Scripture reference, you'll see the text with a number over the words. If you touch the number, it translates the meaning of the word. Why is this important? Because not everything carries over into our English translations perfectly. For instance, there are seven Hebrew words translated *praise* that all have different meanings. Some mean "to play with a musical instrument," while others mean "to bow in reverence" or "to celebrate, make a show, and even be clamorously foolish." Our English translation isn't wrong; it just doesn't have the vocabulary to fit all of that meaning into a single word, so we're stuck with the word *praise* to encompass them all. I use my app often, both to understand what the writer was conveying and also to help move the words from my head to my heart. The more I can engage with what God is saying, the greater the likelihood it will stick in my memory.

Listening to the Bible

Auditory learners may find it helpful to listen to Bible-reading media. When I had an art studio, I listened to readings on CD while working for hours at a time. Not only did it give me something to think about while I was creating but it was great to fill the atmosphere of my studio with the Word of God. While I don't believe listening to Scripture should completely take the place of personal Bible study, it's an amazing tool that our generation has at their fingertips. Some people enjoy dramatized audio recordings with actors and sound effects, while others just enjoy the simple spoken words read out loud. There are lots of options to choose from!

Reading the Bible in a Year

Did you know that you can read the entire Bible in less than a year by reading five chapters a day? If that seems too daunting, find a yearly Bible that is marked by sections that help break it down into bite-sized pieces. I've done this many times, and often I'll use a highlighter to underline the parts that stand out to me during the year.

Getting a New Bible

One way of keeping the Bible fresh is to get a new one every few years. If you're like me, you love to read a Bible until it's practically falling apart. I can flip to my favorite passages easily, and I love the nice worn feeling that comes from a well-read book. However, one day I noticed that I was overlooking passages in my older Bible because my eye was being drawn to highlighted pages, and I was becoming more attached to my familiar book than to God's Word itself. So I put my favorite Bible on the shelf and got a crisp new one that was ready for more highlighting and new studies. As I read, I simply highlighted what I found interesting.

One day while I was working at my job, a client kept asking me questions about the Lord. She was so hungry to know more about faith in Christ, and I answered her questions as best as I knew how to at the moment. Suddenly I felt impressed to give her my Bible, the one I was highlighting and reading through at that moment. She was overwhelmed at the gift, and I prayed that the highlighting and what I had added in the notes would help in her faith journey. It was a great reminder that sometimes it's good to try new things—you never know how God may touch someone's life as a result!

As we look at some of these tools, ask yourself if there are one or two specific ideas that work for you, and then come up with a strategy to implement them into your world. Early morning is a great time to focus on the Word. Some people play music softly in the background, and others prefer silence as they read, so do whatever works for you. The important thing is to start a routine and do it regularly. You'll discover that God has a unique way of bringing things up during the rest of the day that tie into what you've been reading, and you'll probably find opportunities to offer what you've learned to others in your life. As we unpack God's Word, it becomes life-giving both to us and to others!

Your Turn

- How would you describe your connection to God's Word? You can use words like *passionate*, *curious*, *academic*, or even *unsure*.
- What would you like to do to deepen that connection?
- Do any of the tools in this chapter feel like a good fit for you?
- What would be a good plan to start using them?

Spiritual Practice

Take some time for self-reflection: Is there an area of spiritual growth you'd like to achieve or a topic you'd like to learn more about in Scripture? Set aside some time with a pen, paper, high-lighters, and a *Strong's Concordance* or Bible app. Start with prayer, asking the Holy Spirit to teach you and bring you greater awareness of his plan and heart. Then spend some time looking into what the Bible has to say on this topic. Feel free to ask a mentor or your local pastor for some coaching as you study.

If that sounds too daunting, search for a Bible-based devotional about the topic you are drawn to and allow it to speak into your life!

FOUR

Community

A PLACE OF BELONGING

In the early spring of 2020, I set out on an adventure. Moving from California to Texas, my plan was to renovate a family cabin, write a book, and hold worship meetings with a group of believers in the house. Bursting with creative vision, I drove from San Diego in my little Prius with the back seats packed full of curtains, vintage lamps, and gilded mirrors to hang on the walls of my new home.

Shortly after I arrived, the local mayor announced a mandatory shelter-at-home policy due to the COVID-19 virus. All my plans came to a screeching halt, and I found myself completely alone in the cabin . . . in the woods . . . by myself . . . just me and the woodland critters.

No worries, I thought, *this will still work. The local stores are still open, and there's plenty to renovate around the house.*

So I threw my energy into the cabin, hoping to breathe some life into the shabby, outdated spaces. And it worked: project "cabin beautiful" came together delightfully. The difficulty was, the more stylish and homey the house became, the more depressed I felt because there was no one to enjoy it with. When I mustered the courage to overcome my terror of drills and build a wooden table, or when I planted beautiful roses by the porch, no one was there to celebrate the moment with me. The beauty felt unappreciated . . . it needed to be enjoyed by others. The lack of human connection was unnerving. My prayers became frequent and fervent.

"Lord, I love this place," I said, trying not to be ungrateful, "and the space to be creative is great, but I was not prepared for this isolation!"

Thankfully, social media and local friendships helped me survive the temporary season, but the experience reminded me of the power of community. As a creative person sometimes prone to hibernate, I rediscovered how much my soul longs for connection, and even a beautiful log cabin with space to dream was incomplete without it. My soul needed community.

God created human beings to be wired for relationships. It's part of our DNA.

> We talk,
> create,
> express ourselves
> in ways
> that crave
> response.
>
> Just as the body hungers,
> *so our souls*
> *crave community.*

Our divine adventure was meant to be lived alongside others. We walk the road of faith together, offering encouragement, wisdom, and a listening ear to our fellow travelers. Companionship is a soul food we were created to crave.

Starting from Scratch: A Model of Love

For the believer in Jesus, the hunger for healthy community is coupled with a desire for spiritual connection and growth. We've been given a pattern of togetherness found in the Scriptures that offers a picture of close relationships.

- Jesus spent over three years living and traveling with twelve disciples.
- They hiked mountains and went on spiritual retreats together.
- Often they stayed in people's homes.
- He healed outcasts and brought them back into society.
- One of Jesus's first directives to the church after the resurrection was to send his disciples to an upper room in Jerusalem. They lived together for nine days until the Spirit was given at Pentecost.

Community was a way of life for these early believers, and one reason for this revolves around a teaching of Jesus that became a core principle of the early church. Sitting around the table with his disciples, the Lord earnestly said,

> A new commandment I give to you, that you *love one another*; as I have loved you, that you also love one another. By this all will know that you are My disciples, if you have love for one another.
>
> John 13:34–35 (emphasis added)

The early church took this command very seriously, practicing the "law of love" when they gathered together. They modeled it in ways such as washing feet, caring for widows and orphans, taking the Lord's supper each week, and meeting in homes. The call to love extended past their immediate family and was meant to be the signature of their faith: the mark that showed they were Christ's followers. This birthed an atmosphere of proactive, nurturing love and created relationships that lasted a lifetime.

The apostle Paul gives us a glimpse into this type of community. When penning a letter to the church he started, he expresses his heartache at the distance that separates them.

> Dear brothers and sisters, after we were separated from you for a little while (though our hearts never left you), we tried very hard to come back because of our intense longing to see you again.
>
> 1 Thessalonians 2:17 NLT

Practicing the love of Christ brought close, authentic connections and deep, lasting friendships. The Greek word for this idea is *koinonia*, meaning "partnership, participation, communion, fellowship." This fellowship is incredibly fulfilling to the human soul, and even in the seventh century, the early saints described it as "taking great drinks of living water," when they came together for spiritual discussions. For them, it was a natural flow of following the command of Jesus: to learn to love one another as he loved them.

In today's culture, spiritual community doesn't always come easily. Our society thrives on independence: we like creating our own world behind earbuds and screens, trusting only our family members and a few close friends to breach the walls of our personal fortress. The idea of close community doesn't always come naturally. In fact, it can feel unsafe and unsettling to think of allowing others into our lives, even though we see this idea modeled in Scripture.

On the other hand, we have to ask ourselves, *What does it practically mean to follow Jesus within community today? Do we sell everything and travel in groups of twelve? Do we share everything we own, like the early disciples did?* In today's world, those ideas sound a bit extreme! What was culturally acceptable in the first century doesn't necessarily work by modern Western standards.

So for anyone who longs for depth in spiritual connection with believers, spiritual community in this era of history is a unique challenge. Many people long for it, but we're not sure how to do it.

Practicing spiritual community may look different through the ages, but the core still revolves around the command of Jesus: *love one another*. The result can be creative, unique, and even profoundly simple as we explore different ways to share the love of Christ with others.

L'Abri: Community in the Swiss Alps

My brother and I were filming a production in Europe and decided to take a few days off to explore the idea of spiritual community. We booked a couple of nights at L'Abri Fellowship, a faith-based community in Switzerland founded by the late Francis and Edith Schaeffer in 1955, where seekers from around the world gather to ask spiritual questions and pursue a life of faith. The L'Abri community (*l'abri* means "shelter" in French) was founded by a missionary couple and their family who opened their home to seekers who wanted to ask questions about spiritual matters. It first started when their college-age daughter brought friends home to visit and ski at the nearby resorts, but soon many others were drawn to the chalet, where long discussions with Dr. Schaeffer offered insight for personal reflection and growth, and creative hospitality from Edith made everyone feel at home. Eventually, friends opted to move to nearby cabins and help with the work, and the community was formed. Today, people from around the world still visit this unique place where deep conversations are fostered and hospitality thrives.[1]

Traveling to L'Abri was an adventure all its own. I held my breath as the bus rounded hairpin curves, just barely clinging to the side of the mountain as we climbed in elevation. Out the window, the mountainous view of the Alps spread above the valley below, with layers of peaks and stunning vistas to hold our gaze.

Practicing spiritual community

may look different through the

ages, but the core still revolves

around the command of Jesus:

love one another.

When our bus pulled to a stop on the side of the road next to a wooden sign that read *L'Abri*, we jumped out and trekked the short path to beautiful chalet cabins perched on the mountainside. We checked in and made our way to our rooms—mine was up a delightful wooden staircase that creaked as I padded up the old floorboards. Warm, welcoming quilts and a soft bed were waiting as I curiously slipped into my room, wondering what adventures the week would bring.

The next morning, we helped with tasks around the community grounds and joined the staff, interns, and guests for meals. At each table, amid wildflowers and yummy food, the host posed a group question that began an open conversation for anyone who wanted to chime in. The topic may have been about arts, philosophy, or how faith impacts society, and all opinions were treated with graciousness. Talk about a stimulating discussion! Travelers from all over the world came to enjoy a home-cooked meal and meaningful conversations. We watched and engaged with spiritual community at its finest: open dialogue around a beautiful, welcoming table.

On our last day at L'Abri, I was given permission to slip into the original chalet where the Schaeffers had first started these meetings. I had read of the beautiful dinners created from scratch in the kitchen by Edith. This powerhouse woman was so creative that she grew her own vegetables, prepared meals for her family from her mountainside garden, and set the table at mealtime with arrangements of elegant wildflowers and special homey touches. Her hospitality made everyone feel welcome, whether they were her own family or visitors. After dinner, many conversations with Francis were hosted around the living-room fireplace, where bodies were warmed during the chilly Swiss winters, and hearts were touched with the message of God's love and truth.[2] I'd heard the legends . . . now I was excited to see where it had actually happened. Slowly opening the front door, I poked my head into the first room and began to explore.

If I'm honest, I'll admit I was a bit shocked. It was so . . . *normal*. The kitchen was not a gourmet design; in fact, it was rather small by Western standards, and the sitting area was also a bit tight. At first, I was slightly disappointed, but only until I realized what I was seeing.

They used what they had, I marveled, noting the gently worn countertops and simple wooden rooms. *It was ordinary, but their love for people made it beautiful. Anyone could do this . . . even me.*

I walked away from that chalet daring my heart to make a difference with whatever simple things I had. Spiritual community simply requires a heart full of love and a space for people: we can all do that.

Community in Small Spaces: The Backyard Garden

A few years after the experience at L'Abri, I began longing for a way to practice spiritual community. I lived in a cottage (a tiny house, really) in California suburbia, so I didn't have much space to entertain. So I pondered my options and waited for the right opportunity.

The tale unfolded when my landlady decided to refinish a dining room table, and after I showed her some refinishing techniques, it became a fun project to do together. When it was finished, she didn't have a place to put it.

"What if we put the table in the backyard?" I suggested. Since the winter rains in the desert region had already passed, she agreed to move the table outside, and the idea worked perfectly.

Surrounded by orange and lemon trees, the table became a delightful spot. Not only did it give me space to host guests but it offered a great key for fun community: *beautiful spaces make people feel safe, special, and loved.* By setting a beautiful table, I could invite people into a space that immediately opened them up to community, because they felt cherished by sitting in a place created for them. At those table dinners, many moments of healing, prayer, and honest conversation happened in the lives of the guests, and true *koinonia* was experienced.

I allowed my heart to dream up ideas with the table. Soon there was a large rug beneath it, a pergola with climbing plants above it, strands of twinkle lights, pots of flowers, china, and silver candlesticks I found at thrift stores. I set the table with any theme I chose, using fresh flowers from the local grocery store and a home-cooked meal.

People would enter the garden with a little gasp, wondering whether this beauty was really for them. One girl said, "It's like stepping into Narnia!"

Another friend said, "Rebecca, it's like you create a three-dimensional piece of art and invite us to step inside."

The beautiful table was the opener. What happened next was key: I steered the conversation toward spiritual topics by asking each person to tell what God was currently teaching them. Often, I started by sharing what he was showing me, offering both an honest struggle and how faith in Christ was bringing me through. Some people shared very little, and others were just waiting for the chance to be heard and had a lot to say. I affirmed what they were saying and told what I loved about it, and in this way, they felt even more comfortable to open up their hearts in a safe place.

After our meal, with candles burning low and crickets chirping in the background, I asked how I could pray for the guests. As they spoke from their hearts, tears were shed, burdens were lifted, and people were encouraged during that time of prayer. God moved in such a unique way that many people simply didn't want to leave the table.

Today I have a larger house with a proper dining room, but I still hear from people who were deeply touched by those times in the orchard. Spiritual community doesn't have to involve a lot of money or time. Anyone can create a space and invite others into the simple joy of conversation about God. Love speaks loudly, and when we find creative ways to offer the love of Jesus to others, community simply happens.

Building Your Table

Hospitality is one way to create a safe place for spiritual community, and when we steer the conversation toward spiritual matters, it creates an opportunity to learn from each other and grow. We realize we're not alone in our struggles, and we practice the love of Christ as we rally around one another, listening and meeting the felt needs in prayer.

> We share honestly.
> We ask for help.
> We become partners
> in the spiritual journey
> of following Christ.

One way to practice this is to create a beautiful table and invite people to a meal. It's an innovative way to invite people into a safe place for community. You can do this for friends, relatives, or even people you would like to get acquainted with. It's just one of the ways we can show people we care and provide a way for fellowship to take place. Here are a few pointers if you want to try it yourself:

- **When setting the table, let yourself dream.** Go thrift shopping, borrow your grandma's silver, make place cards, use your good dishes. The table doesn't have to be outside—you can do it anywhere. Make it special, and even look online for inspiration or a theme.

- **If you're not creative, grill steaks!** Let's face it, not all of us have that creative gift as strong as others, but you can find ways to create a special meal that others appreciate. Doing something special is the goal, so figure out a way

Love speaks loudly,
and when we find
creative ways to offer
the love of Jesus
to others, community
simply happens.

that works for you. Make a meal that others will appreciate, even if you have to make it simple.

- **Invite the guests.** Pray about who to invite to your dinner. Sometimes the person you least expect might be exactly the right one who would be deeply touched by a beautiful meal. Your selection of guests will affect the dinner conversation and tone of the evening, so thoughtfully consider who would be the right ones to ask.

- **Prepare for the conversation.** When you invite them, make sure people know that you're having both food and a deeper spiritual conversation. If they're prepared, they'll be much more ready to flow with the idea than if you spring it on them in the moment.

- **Set the tone with prayer.** I've discovered that praying specifically over each chair at the table before people arrive makes a huge impact. Sometimes I invite a friend to come early and pray with me, and we take a small flask of oil and anoint each chair, asking the Lord to enable the guests to receive his love in a special way. It's amazing how the Holy Spirit moves when we invite him to!

- **Ask for help.** On a practical note, ask for help with the dishes and cleanup *before* the day of the dinner. People are happy to help, but they need to be asked, so make sure you have a friend or two lined up to stay afterward. Otherwise you may be up late cleaning all by yourself.

Simple Community

If the idea of creating a beautiful table is not your style, here are a few other simple ideas for practicing community:

- Meet with a friend or two for coffee to talk and pray together.

- Schedule a monthly session with a mentor.
- Consider mentoring someone younger in the faith.
- Look for small groups or "life groups" within your church that offer weekly community meetings.
- Create ways to honor and thank the spiritual leaders in your life.
- Join a Bible study and see if people want to meet afterward for a meal and spiritual discussion.
- Look for a church that is intentionally building community life within their programs and opportunities.

Be gentle on yourself and others in the process. Not everyone may want to embrace spiritual community like you do, but keep reaching out and looking for ways to make it happen. Remember that practicing spiritual community is simply carrying out the command of Jesus to love other believers. When you find a place to do that well, you fulfill his command, and a divine adventure unfolds.

Your Turn

- Outside of your immediate family, do you feel like you have a good spiritual community?
- What are some important things to you within a spiritual community?
- Do you feel like this type of community is easy to find?
- How are you practicing the command of Jesus to "love one another"?

Spiritual Practice

Find a means of cultivating community in a fresh way. Host a dinner, go to a retreat with a group, find a friend to have coffee with, or have a chat with someone you haven't spoken with for a while. When you do, think of how you can offer love in a special way. Maybe it's offering to pray with someone or extending a helping hand to someone else who is creating a community setting. Look for a creative way to connect with others that also honors Christ!

FIVE

Forgiveness

DEMONSTRATING GRACE TO OTHERS

I'm sitting on a cozy sofa as I write these words to you, my reader friend, tucked away in a scenic log home surrounded by rich pine forest. Warm wood tones like rich honey . . . a tall stone fireplace . . . a wraparound porch with a hot tub—it's the perfect spot for a writer's retreat. Aside from the soft ticking of a clock, it's completely quiet.

But I didn't reserve this place online or rent it for a weekend. This cabin recently belonged to my father, and the reason I'm sitting here today involves a tale of forgiveness, restoration, and a choice to love. For many years, this had been Dad's solace, a peaceful place of refuge. It became such a big part of him that, against the protests of his family, he opted to stay in the cabin rather than move to an assisted living home.

Just a few short months ago, I sat in this living room next to his mechanical bed. Hospice care had arranged for his last days to be spent in the beautiful log home. When he slipped into an unconscious state, I was privileged to be with him during the last two hours of his life on earth, praying and singing worship songs next to his propped-up, silent body.

> I held his hand.
> Cried.
> Prayed.
> Sang him songs
> we'd sung together.
>
> Then he was gone—
> finally free
> from the body
> that plagued him
> with pain.

In the warmth of the cabin, surrounded by hospice workers and the long-distance support of family members, my dad went home to be with Jesus. I still cry when I think about it: the sacred moment, when love was at its raw state. When tears and snot and grief and relief and joy were all spun together in a wad of thick emotion. Humans wept, but angels rejoiced. I could feel it all.

The depth of that moment was compounded by the unusual elements of my father's life. After a car accident that resulted in his traumatic brain injury when I was a child, his mental abilities were greatly damaged. He was even arrested and imprisoned for child abuse when I was eleven years of age, and my adolescence was spent estranged from a father whose mental health was unstable at best. Many years later, when our relationship was restored, I considered him a close friend and helped take care of him during the last years of his life. For me, this cabin is more than a beautiful place: each time I step on the property, I'm reminded of the practice of forgiveness and how crucial it is to a divine adventure of faith.

The Power of Forgiveness

The *Huffington Post* published an article entitled "The Power of Forgiveness" that stated,

> Forgiveness means giving up the suffering of the past and being willing to forge ahead with far greater potential for inner freedom. Besides the reward of letting go of a painful past, there are powerful health benefits that go hand-in-hand with the practice of forgiveness. . . .
>
> In the physical domain, forgiveness is associated with lower heart rate and blood pressure as well as overall stress relief. It is also associated with improving physical symptoms, reducing fatigue in some patient populations, and improving sleep quality.
>
> In the psychological domain, forgiveness has been shown to diminish the experience of stress and inner conflict while simultaneously restoring positive thoughts, feelings, and behaviors.[1]

In today's society, it's easy to recognize the healthy need to let the past go or give someone another chance, since the physical and emotional health benefits of releasing offenses can be proven with science. But as believers in Christ, we recognize that forgiveness affects not only our souls and bodies but also our spiritual life. Intentionally forgiving the faults of others and receiving forgiveness for our shortcomings is crucial for healthy Christianity.

One of the quickest ways to grow closer to God is to cultivate intentional forgiveness in our daily lives: it's like using Miracle-Gro for our spiritual life! The opposite is also true: one of the biggest ways a person can stifle a life of faith is to choose to hold on to anger and bitterness. Harboring unforgiveness is like feeding your soul arsenic: you cannot be spiritually healthy if you allow this poison to remain in your heart.

A Paid Debt

The value of forgiveness is high. Sometimes the cost is too. If we choose to forgive, we have to invite God into moments we'd often rather forget. The sting of betrayal . . . the grief of someone who *should have* but *didn't* . . . maybe the person we need to forgive the most is ourselves. Graciously, our Lord peels back the layers of bandages wound around the damaged parts of our souls. He sees. He knows. He feels the hurt. He's been there too.

In his kindness, Jesus never minimizes the pain that's associated with an offense. He doesn't ask us to brush offenses under the rug and hope things work out . . . to turn a blind eye to the faults of others . . . or to become a doormat for them to walk on. We know this because God didn't say this to us. When humankind turned away and rejected his plan, God *didn't* say, "I know you mess up sometimes, but that's okay because you're human and I understand."

Instead, he faced the pain of the offense head-on . . . and it took him to the cross.

Before Christ came, we were cut off from God, fully estranged from our Father. The wide gap between earth and heaven was irreversible unless the debt was paid. Our sin separates us from a holy God. There is no way to deal with this wound lightly. Jesus knew that the relationship was broken, but he didn't brush off our sin or offer false hopes. Instead, as fully man and fully God, Jesus came to take responsibility and do the hard work required to heal this relationship between heaven and earth. Even if it cost his life.

Christ suffered the pain from a broken relationship caused by hurt and betrayal. He poignantly pointed out false beliefs that keep us from truly connecting to God's heart. And he made it personal: bearing the pain that should have been ours to wear for eternity. Jesus bled and wept, was falsely accused by the justice system, and suffered the worst kind of anguish by human hands. Finally, the King of Heaven was crucified with thieves and robbers. As the crowd jeered and mocked, he gasped, "Father, forgive them. They don't know what they are doing."

It should have been me. And you. But it wasn't.

This God-man made a choice. As God, he shouldered the hot mess of humanity, bore the death penalty we deserved, and paid the debt between us and God. As human, he made the tough choice to forgive.

> Done deal.
> Forgiven.
>
> The sting of death—
> Gone.
>
> Fear of hell—
> Over.
>
> Forgiveness—
> Granted
>   to everyone
>   who asks.

Oh, the joy! Hallelujah! Our debt is paid and we are free to receive the Father's love. Imagine $100,000 of credit card debt instantly gone, or a lifelong prison sentence dismissed . . . those would be reasons to celebrate. Forgiveness of sin is far greater . . . our Benefactor's gift extends into eternity. The weight of sin is gone, and a new life of freedom begins.

God's forgiveness comes with a requirement—that we forgive others too. That we extend the grace that has been given to us.

> We don't ignore the pain
> because God never did.
>
> He sees our hurt.
> He knows the pain
> of being broken.
>
> Instead, we stare it in the face
> Daring to do the hard work
> Processing through the pain
> Choosing to forgive.

And we have his help.

Always.

Life with Father—My Forgiveness Story

Dad loved the forest. When I was growing up, he loved building tree forts for us to play in and entertaining guests in our home in the rolling hills of Wisconsin. He read stacks of books to his kids, built campfires and carved sticks for roasting hot dogs, and wanted to pass his Christian faith on to his children. Some of my first memories of Dad are watching him sit up late in the hallway with his Bible and notebook, studying the Scriptures and making sure my siblings and I didn't sneak out of bed after hours.

The Christmas Day when I was nine years old, my whole family was in a car accident while driving home from a holiday dinner. Our car spun out of control and careened into a ditch in the snowy countryside, and my father, brother, and I were thrown from the back seat and hurled into the frigid air. When the car came to a screeching halt, my mom turned around from her front seat to see if we were okay, but there was nobody there.

My memory has blocked out this moment, but I'm told my face was covered with blood as I lay in the field. Dad was silent—his head hit the pavement and he immediately slipped into a coma. The grass was strewn with toys and Christmas gifts . . . months later we were still finding them near the site of the wreckage.

When I woke up in the hospital, my face was sore from stitches. Plastic surgery had been needed to remove shards of broken glass, and my legs hurt from fractured bones. Thankfully, I completely recovered after weeks in the hospital and several months of healing at home.

My dad had the hardest road to recovery. When he opened his eyes after two weeks in a coma, we discovered that his mental and emotional states were completely altered. I remember talking to this confused stranger who was supposed to be my father . . . not knowing how to process the situation. After months of rehab, we went home to a life that would never be the same. Dad flew into fits of rage and sometimes became physically violent toward his children.

Eventually my mom called the police. I still remember officers arriving at the house and taking him away . . . it was the last time he ever came home. Our supervised meetings with him were strained and awkward. When I was a teenager, my mom moved my siblings and me to Texas, away from the drama, where we could start a new life. Soon we stopped visiting Dad, and I didn't see him for eight years. It was a merciful end to the chaos.

People would ask me whether I had forgiven my dad, and I'd obediently nod. After all, it wasn't his fault. He didn't plan the car accident or even recognize when his hostile moods swung out of control. But I knew it wasn't healthy to rebuild a relationship with a person who would only hurt me. I just sort of moved on in life without my father, having the vague feeling that I was missing out on something vastly valuable. But I had no way of fixing the broken pieces.

Doing the Work

On the cusp of adulthood, some dear friends invested many hours into my healing journey, gently pulling the shrapnel from my soul. I cried buckets of tears, sometimes not even knowing why I was crying, and slowly some of the numbness started to fade. Repeatedly, they challenged me to forgive, even when I thought I already had. I remember one phone conversation with my mentor.

"Rebecca," she said boldly, "I was praying for you and just really feel like you need to search your heart and make *sure* you've forgiven. Because of God's calling on your life, you can't afford to have *any* bitterness in your heart."

Her honest comment stung because I thought I *had* forgiven, but I searched my heart and made an extra effort to have a clean slate when it came to my family. I chose to confront places of pain head-on rather than hiding them. I talked about memories with my mentors and allowed Christ to bring healing. And I trusted God with the rest, giving him my pain and forgiving my father the best I knew how.

At the time, I was recording a collection of songs. One friend said, "I think you should give a copy to your dad."

"No," I quickly responded, "that wouldn't be healthy."

But after thinking about it, I decided to give it a try. *It would be terrible if something happened to Dad*, I thought, *and I hadn't reached out at all.*

I wrote a note and mailed a CD, which led to a phone call. A few months later, a family member passed away and I went to Wisconsin for the funeral. Dad and I decided to meet at a little café. I still remember being nervous and a little scared of encountering that angry, defensive man I had known as a child.

What I discovered shocked me: Dad's hard facade had mellowed, and somewhere behind the slightly disheveled clothes and overgrown beard was the most tender, loving father I could imagine. He was so kind during our meeting, and so openly in love with Jesus. It was like talking with an old friend after a long distance. God had been working in his heart too.

Two years later, Dad came to visit us in Texas over Thanksgiving. In the hotel room with my brothers and me, he said the words that changed our relationship forever.

"I just want to clear the air," he said. "I've sinned against God and you guys. Will you forgive me?"

The room was pin-drop quiet, charged with emotion. We never imagined receiving an apology from our father. Shocked, I was just able to get words past the massive lump in my throat.

"Dad," I said, "I already have."

We both cried.

I hadn't forgiven Dad because I was trying to feel better about myself or get anything from him. In fact, I didn't think I would ever speak to him again. I forgave him because I wanted to be right with God. Then, when he owned his issues and asked for my forgiveness, I discovered God had already done the needed work for me to extend mercy and kindness in return. Practicing forgiveness, simply because Christ has forgiven me and commanded me to forgive, opened the door for healing when the moment was right.

Pay It Forward

Jesus's disciples often struggled with the practice of forgiveness. In Matthew 18, Peter came to Jesus and said, "Lord, how often shall my brother sin against me, and I forgive him? Up to seven times?" (v. 21).

During those days, Jewish rabbis taught that a person only needed to forgive their brother three times, so Peter may have thought he was being generous to offer seven opportunities for forgiveness.

"I do not say to you, up to seven times," responded Jesus, "but up to seventy times seven" (v. 22).

How astonished Peter must have been when Jesus raised the bar even higher! Then the Lord followed his statement with a story that illustrated why the practice of forgiveness is required by God.

Therefore the kingdom of heaven is like a certain king who wanted to settle accounts with his servants. And when he had begun to settle accounts, one was brought to him who owed him ten thousand talents. But as he was not able to pay, his master commanded that he be sold, with his wife and children and all that he had, and that payment be made. The servant therefore fell down before him, saying, "Master, have patience with me, and I will pay you all." Then the master of that servant was moved with compassion, released him, and forgave him the debt.

But that servant went out and found one of his fellow servants who owed him a hundred denarii; and he laid hands on him and took him by the throat, saying, "Pay me what you owe!" So his fellow servant fell down at his feet and begged him, saying, "Have patience with me, and I will pay you all." And he would not, but went and threw him into prison till he should pay the debt. So when his fellow servants saw what had been done, they were very grieved, and came and told their master all that had been done. Then his master, after he had called him, said to him, "You wicked servant! I forgave you all that debt because you begged me. Should you not also have had compassion on your fellow servant, just as I had pity on you?" And his master was angry, and delivered him to the torturers until he should pay all that was due to him.

So My heavenly Father also will do to you if each of you, from his heart, does not forgive his brother his trespasses.

Matthew 18:23–35

Forgiveness is not just a good idea that will make us feel better or a self-help technique to help us cope with past pain. It's a command from God with a warning: if we don't extend the kindness of God, it won't come back to us.

God has forgiven us an infinitely greater debt than anyone on earth could owe us, and he asks us to pay it forward and forgive others.

Part of our spiritual journey as a follower of Christ is to really work through the issues of our heart in light of what Jesus has done for us. We're not just forgiving for the sake of ourselves or someone else—as followers of Jesus, we recognize that God is requiring us to pass on the forgiveness we've received from him.

The Refuge Cabin

The story gets better. Dad and I learned to laugh together. He bought me my first camera. He earned my trust and love through being consistently present and respectful. He still walked with a limp due to the head injury, struggled with his memory, and had a lot of funny quirks. But he loved me, and I was able to receive his love and give back.

90

Eventually I discovered a beautiful log cabin for sale about twenty minutes from my house in Texas. Dad bought it, and for the next twelve years, the cabin was a place of refuge for him and everyone who set foot in the door. I helped him decorate and maintain the cabin, and even lived with him for several years in between film and ministry trips. We held home groups in the cabin, we hosted missionaries, and visitors were often struck by the tangible peace of God when they walked through the door.

Dad was constantly worshiping God . . . in the cabin, at the grocery store, or at the mall . . . he didn't care who was watching. He was so grateful for God's goodness that his face would light up with a smile of praise and he'd raise his hands and worship whenever he felt the urge.

I'd like to say that everything was perfect in our relationship, but it was still difficult at times since Dad's injury had left permanent damage to his brain and he didn't always process his emotions well. There were times I had to practice forgiveness and times I had to ask him to forgive me for my response. Yet we were always close, and I'm amazed that God was able to take a relationship that was so broken and make it whole again. When we let go of our pain and trust God with the results, he can do amazing things.

The Father Restores

The apostle Paul found himself in the middle of an odd relationship triangle with his friend Philemon, a house church pastor who had ministered with Paul, and his runaway slave named Onesimus. (During the first century, many believers like Philemon freed their slaves, and others treated them like family members, although the Roman Empire encouraged slavery.) Onesimus had run away from Philemon, probably stealing money, and had somehow met the apostle Paul. They had become dear friends and Onesimus had converted to Christianity, yet the new slave-turned-believer's conscience was pricking him—even though he was free, he felt it was his Christian duty to go back to his owner and repay any debts that he had left. This was a risky idea, since runaway slaves were beaten and often branded with hot irons if caught. Taking responsibility for the wrongdoing could come with a high price.

Picking up his pen, the apostle Paul opted to wield his relationship as a mentor to weigh in on the situation. "I thank my God," he wrote to Philemon, the master of this slave, "making mention of you always in my prayers" (Philem. 4).

Making a plea for the runaway's case, he asked Philemon to receive the slave on behalf of their close friendship and the grace of God. "But if he has wronged you or owes anything, put that on my account. I, Paul, am writing with my own hand. I will repay," Paul vowed (Philem. 18–19).

Tradition says that Philemon listened to the apostle Paul and forgave the former slave. This short letter offers us a practical demonstration of love from the first century: a plea for forgiveness based on the grace of God.

One day I was reading these verses and began to look at the words a bit deeper. *What if this letter had been written to me?* I wondered. *If someone who had broken my trust and robbed me of something precious brought me a letter from a spiritual guide asking me to forgive for their sake, would I do it?* I'd probably opt for forgiveness, not only out of Christian duty but out of respect for my mentor.

Suddenly I sensed the Lord prompting me, *What if I wrote you this letter? Suppose I came to you asking, for the sake of our friendship, that you forgive someone who wronged you?*

I realized then that Paul's letter is a picture of what Jesus asks when someone wrongs us. He never reasons away their guilt or denies the hurt that they have caused. Instead, he asks us to forgive them for his sake. Because of our relationship with Christ, he asks us to pardon the ones who have wronged us.

Then he goes a step further: *If your offender owes you anything, put that on my account. I will repay.*

If Paul the apostle was gracious enough to offer repayment to Philemon for anything his runaway slave had stolen, how much more is our Father in heaven willing to repay any debt owed to us? He owns the entire universe and is fully able to restore the things that are broken in our lives if we just release them and "put the debt on his account." If Jesus gave his very life to save us, won't he also restore stolen things if we ask? Are we willing to fully forgive those who have wronged us and "put the debt on Jesus"?

I've discovered that this idea is a powerful key to the forgiveness process. When I feel the awkward stab of hurt from a betrayal, I take a moment to step aside and spend some time with the Lord.

"Father," I pray, "I choose to forgive this person because of how you've shown me mercy."

Then I take a quick inventory of what I felt robbed of. Was my self-worth robbed? Did I feel used or taken advantage of? Am I feeling the loss of a friendship? Whatever it is, I know that my Father in heaven desires wholeness and restoration for me. With this in mind, I'll pray, "Lord, I put these needs on your account and ask you to meet them. I believe you are a good Father who delights to give us good gifts."

I can't tell you how many times God has responded to this prayer in my life! By shifting my expectations from humans, who are not always trustworthy, to focus on God, whose very name is Faithful and True, I'm practicing forgiveness and creating an opportunity for Christ to restore in his way and time. Our Father in heaven loves to restore. He delights in rewarding us for choosing to look like Jesus, even when it's hard. He is the dance partner who is *always* ready to take our hand. He just is.

The Rest of the Story

Thirty years after the car accident, almost to the day, I drove my father to the local emergency room. On Christmas Eve, his doctor

Are we willing to
fully forgive those who
have wronged us and
"put the debt on Jesus"?
I've discovered that this
idea is a powerful key to
the forgiveness process.

had called in response to a checkup visit: "The results of his blood-work are very concerning. Take him to the emergency room."

Four days later, Dad came home on hospice care. His body was simply worn out after three decades of pain. We set up a bed in the cabin he loved and started 24/7 care. I stayed for a couple of weeks to help him get situated and then got sick myself, so I flew back to my home in California to rest from the unplanned stretch of caregiving. One morning I called Dad over video chat. He had lost his ability to speak, but I could still read his lips.

"I can't breathe," he mouthed.

"It's okay, Dad," I told him, holding back the tears. "You're just getting really close to being with Jesus. I'm a little jealous because you get to see him before I do! You just rest and focus on him."

He smiled and looked up, like he was seeing an invisible light.

A few minutes later I got the phone call from the hospice nurse in Texas: "If anyone wants to see your dad, they need to come," she said. "He's fixin' to go."

I found a flight and packed in an hour, arriving that night after he'd slipped into a coma. He passed the next morning as I was singing and praying next to his bedside. There's no doubt in my mind that my father is dancing with Jesus in heaven, fully whole and free from his broken body.

Most times we forgive just because it's the right thing to do: we forgive because we choose to honor Christ. Every now and then we witness restoration in relationships because of our choice to forgive, and this brings joy to us on earth. Sometimes we experience the rewards that only God can give as a result of tenacious forgiveness with the help of Christ.

I'm writing from my dad's cabin today because he left it to me just before he passed away. The forest home that I helped choose and decorate for Dad is now a quiet place where I can write and host worship meetings of my own. If I had chosen to harden my heart and refuse to explore the idea of forgiving my dad, I would not be sitting in this beautiful cabin today. When God calls us to forgive, he knows what he's talking about.

The adventure of forgiveness will look different in your story than it does in mine. You'll have your own valleys of pain and mountaintops of monumental blessing as God responds to your choice to forgive. Practicing forgiveness simply offers another opportunity to connect with Jesus in the divine adventure he has for your life. Even personal pain can become a means to build connection with the One we love, causing us to look more like Jesus as we follow his steps to the adventure he has for us.

Your Turn

- Have you been forgiven by God for your sins? If so, thank him! If not, spend a little time asking Jesus to forgive you, removing the gulf between you and the Father.
- Do you find it difficult to forgive others? Explain.
- Is there anyone you need to forgive? Write a list.
- Ask God to help you forgive others, even when it's hard.

Spiritual Practice

Write a list of people who have wronged you, and ask God to help you forgive. Here are some tips:

- Feel free to express your emotions as you write by penning how the situation made you feel. Specifically write what was "stolen" from you.
- Spend some time in prayer and lay your list before the Lord, telling him that you choose to forgive each person for the specific wounds they inflicted in your life.

- Ask the Father to "put on his account" everything that was stolen from you, since he is a good Father and desires to see us whole. Thank him, and trust that he has heard your prayer.

Suggested prayer:

I acknowledge the pain I experienced from _____, and I am deciding to extend the love of Jesus in this situation because of how deeply I am loved by him. I place on the account of Christ everything that was stolen from me, such as _____, because I know you love to meet my needs. Thank you, Father, for forgiving my sins and enabling me to forgive the sins of others.

Note: In the time between writing this chapter and publishing the book, the cabin has been fully restored for use as a retreat and worship center. Guests have come from many miles away, hundreds of lives have been touched, and my dad's legacy of worship thrives in the peaceful space he left behind.

SIX

Pilgrimage

THE LOST ART OF ADVENTURING WITH GOD

I learned about pilgrimage the summer I traveled to Ireland on a one-way ticket. Cameras in hand, I kissed American soil goodbye and reveled in the timeless beauty of the British Isles for six weeks to create a documentary. I didn't have a full schedule. My calendar had penciled-in ideas, but there was a daunting amount of white space. The idea was to create a film about the early Celtic saints, traveling within Northern Ireland, the Republic of Ireland, Scotland, and England to follow the steps of these passionate men and women whose faith shone brightly during the Dark Ages. My heart was both terrified and thrilled as I dared myself to dream about how God might fill the time with adventures. It was a journey with him, and I couldn't wait to see what he would do.

Within a few days of my landing on the Emerald Isle, an unusual string of events unfolded. It was shocking to see how fast my calendar filled up. I found myself sitting with poets, archaeologists, authors, historians, and people who simply had a strong dose of

Highland hospitality and generously offered to drive me to Celtic ruins, stone abbeys, and ancient sites that helped my research. I felt so alive! Every time another "coincidental" meeting happened, my faith was stirred to recognize that God was guiding this journey and blessing my path. During the first four weeks of my trip, I had only two days to rest.

By the end of the trip, my faith was much richer. I realized that the blank spaces in my calendar were great opportunities for God to handwrite engagements with people I would have never met without mustering the courage to put my feet on foreign soil. I bonded with new friends. The land felt alive, and my faith was nourished by stories of passionate saints who had lived long before my time. The price of living out of suitcases for a few weeks was completely outweighed by the beauty I experienced along the way.

Later I discovered that my experience was not so unusual. The truth is, God likes to meet with people who make pilgrimages. While it requires a sacrifice of time and comfort, the price pales in comparison to the life-changing experiences that can occur as we create a space for God to show up in our lives. Whether we're taking a trip around the world or finding a nearby location to visit, taking a journey and inviting God helps us embrace a divine adventure that can build our faith in beautiful ways.

Through the ages, adventuring with God has been expressed by this little-known word: *pilgrimage.*

Wikipedia defines *pilgrimage* this way: "A pilgrimage is a journey, often into an unknown or foreign place, where a person goes in search of new or expanded meaning about their self, others, nature, or a higher good, through the experience . . . after which the pilgrim returns to their daily life."[1]

Christian pilgrimage often revolves around a destination holy site or a place that inspires our faith, like a trip to Israel to walk where Jesus walked. However, sometimes we find that taking a pilgrimage is really about stepping out of our normal, comfortable world to engage with Christ on a fun adventure. The people we meet and truths we discover about ourselves and God are just a few things we gain along the journey. Making a pilgrimage is another exciting way to spend quality time with God. It often involves walking paths set aside for pilgrims that have been trod by other saints for hundreds or thousands of years.

Modern-Day Pilgrim

Blue-green water with hints of turquoise lapped against the sides of the Caledonian MacBrayne ferry, and I leaned over the railing to breathe the crisp, salty air. My film trip and personal pilgrimage was building momentum as several creative friends joined me to film in Scotland, and we continued to plant our feet in the steps of the early saints.

Our destination: Iona, an ancient island that has been considered a holy site. During the Middle Ages, Iona was the center of Gaelic Christianity for the British Isles, and even pagan Viking kings who raided this island ended up converting to Christianity and chose to be buried there upon death. While the island's population is only 177 today, 130,000 tourists visit each year, believing the island still carries a whiff of past prayers and sacred spaces that can be touched by modern hands.

My friend Rolinke, an author and Scottish missionary, was also traveling to Iona on the ferry. When the boat docked, we interviewed each other: I asked her questions about the book she was writing on modern-day pilgrimage, and she quizzed me about what brought me to the island as a film producer. We met for tea in a private garden overlooking the sea, and I discovered her to be a deep well of information about the fascinating history and art of pilgrimage.

"Would you define the idea of 'pilgrimage' for us?" I asked. "It's a word that's not used very much these days—at least not where I come from."

"It has been a very common thing to do, especially in medi-eval times," Rolinke began, unpacking her passion for this term, "and the church was really trying to get people to do pilgrimages, because they believed it would bring you closer to heaven. They walked on foot to Jerusalem, Rome, or traveled by boat to Iona, wanting to get their lives right with God or receive healing."

I glanced out to sea, silenced by the thought of thousands of pilgrims who still come to this island, hoping for a glimpse of God. An ancient site of saints and kings, Iona seemed to be a magnet for seekers, even today. The idea of taking a spiritual journey was still compelling many to visit this tiny, mysterious island.

"When I was a child," Rolinke continued, "pilgrims were our heroes. I grew up hearing stories of their adventures and being inspired by their faith. I discovered that I, too, was a traveler who loved discovering new places around the world, but I also loved finding God and a deeper understanding of myself along the way. It helped form my life, build my faith, and I discovered a passion for pilgrimage."

"Tell me about modern pilgrims," I said, intrigued by the revival of this ancient practice. "Do people still walk the trails now?"

"In Europe we have many pilgrim roads that people are walking today," Rolinke replied. "People are looking for spirituality, healing, rest, identity . . . literally, the road beside our house is a pilgrim road and we meet many people who are actively walking the trails."

I was astonished! I had no idea that thousands of people still practiced this idea, but after spending the day on Iona, I could tell why. Meeting island residents, connecting with the Christian history on the island, and walking its quiet beaches made the day an incredible experience.

> For centuries,
> the island had
> been soaked in
> constant prayer.

> It seemed the rocks
> were crying out
> to testify
> of all they'd seen.

A pilgrim heart absorbs the stories of faith found on sites where they actually happened. Our faith is strengthened when we touch the stones and walk the ground where God moved in ages past. We can hear about it from books or the mouths of others, but when we *go* . . . when we challenge ourselves to meet with God on the journey . . . the events embed themselves in our minds and become real to us. God moves us from the stories we hear to the stories we live out. Taking a pilgrimage becomes a beautiful way to embrace the divine adventure of faith and make it our own.

The History of Pilgrimage

The Scriptures tell us a lot about pilgrimage. In the New Testament, the Greek word for *pilgrim* means "to be a resident foreigner." The word comes from two words meaning "to be near" and "to make oneself at home in a foreign country, to reside, be a stranger." It's that sense of being in a country that's not your home but coming alongside what's happening in that place. In the case of making a pilgrimage, you're stepping into unfamiliar territory because of something special you hope to discover along the way. You're coming near to God during the journey, even though you're away from your normal home.

In the Old Testament, the Israelites were commanded to take a pilgrimage three times a year to Jerusalem in order to worship at the temple.[2] The feasts of Passover, Pentecost, and Tabernacles required all the men to travel from around the country for a spiritual journey. Sometimes entire families traveled together, and caravans from around the nation streamed to the city for worship, prayer, and giving of gifts. Since the presence of God dwelt at the temple,

Hebrew pilgrims were literally leaving their homes to go meet with him. Leaving their land and houses behind, they embraced the life of a pilgrim for a few days while meeting with God in worship. It was such a time of joy that the Psalms record,

> Blessed is the man whose strength is in You,
> Whose heart is set on pilgrimage. . . .
> They go from strength to strength;
> Each one appears before God in Zion.
>
> Psalm 84:5, 7

In the New Testament, we see Jesus and the apostles carrying on this idea of pilgrimage.

- Twelve-year-old Jesus was found in the temple reasoning with the leaders during a pilgrimage to Jerusalem.[3]
- As an adult, he often left Galilee in the north of Israel to travel to feasts in the city.[4]
- God sent the Holy Spirit on Pentecost, when people from many nations were in Jerusalem on pilgrimage for the feast.[5]
- The apostle Paul traveled to Jerusalem to keep a feast.[6]

After the temple was destroyed in AD 70, this pattern of pilgrimage for temple worship ceased. Believers in Christ didn't worship God at a destination, because they embraced the presence of God in their own lives by the leading of the Holy Spirit. Yet, the idea of pilgrimage remained, since many of the disciples were constantly being sent out on missionary journeys and often remained on the move during times of persecution. Some of them even used the term *pilgrim* to describe their lifestyle as followers of Christ; their true home was in heaven and they simply were ready to go anywhere he led them while on earth.

For hundreds of years, a feeling of homelessness crept into the persecuted church, and they began to identify even more with the lifestyle of a pilgrim. It wasn't comfortable, easy, or safe to be a Christian, and they often reminded themselves how earth was not their real home.

> Beloved, I beg you as sojourners and pilgrims, abstain from fleshly lusts which war against the soul.
>
> 1 Peter 2:11

> These all died in faith, not having received the promises, but having seen them afar off were assured of them, embraced them and confessed that they were strangers and pilgrims in the earth.
>
> Hebrews 11:13

After the Roman emperor Constantine legalized Christianity, believers felt safe in their own homes again, but the idea of pilgrimage continued to thrive. Many took trips into the wilderness of Egypt and Arabia to receive mentoring by the Desert Fathers and Mothers who created little communities devoted to prayer. Throughout the Middle Ages, the church encouraged people to take pilgrimages to encounter God in Jerusalem, Rome, Iona, and elsewhere. Taking a spiritual journey encouraged people to put their faith to the test by leaving the comfort of their homes to encounter God. Taking a pilgrimage became a badge of honor, and many people risked the dangers of solitary travel in order to fulfill this mission of taking a spiritual journey.

In modern times, the trend toward pilgrimage in popular culture is coming back around. The most popular trail, the Camino de Santiago in Spain, has over three hundred thousand pilgrims each year. Many people walk simply for personal enjoyment, but others come for deeper reasons: to grieve the death or separation from a loved one or to learn more about themselves in the stillness of the long walk. Other pilgrimages include trips to the Holy Land of Israel, which enable Christians to visit sites connected to their faith. Some have powerful experiences with God, while others simply take away a greater understanding of the historical context of the Bible.

Why Practice Pilgrimage?

In the Western world, it's easy for us to do what the early church didn't have the luxury of doing: *get comfortable*. We have homes with soft beds, enough food, and a social life that brings us emotional stability. Many of us don't really *need* God in our daily lives—we don't have to trust him for each meal or to guide us each day. Going on a pilgrimage moves us from our *normal*. Distractions disperse, and suddenly our focus is completely on God.

> In traveling
> we center
> our souls
> on Christ.
>
> We tune into
> our Home
> that's bigger than
> the place we live,
> our job, and family.
>
> We listen,
> unwind,
> and find again
> our heart's rhythm,
> drawing near to God,
> and him to us.

Unlike the Old Testament believers, we don't have to travel to Jerusalem to be in God's presence, because Christ dwells in our hearts by faith. Yet, we can encounter the Holy Spirit in really beautiful ways as we "set our hearts on pilgrimage" and take an adventure with him. The people we meet and the experiences we have on a pilgrimage will last a lifetime.

Going on a pilgrimage
moves us from our *normal*.
Distractions disperse,
and suddenly our focus
is completely on God.

Close to Home

Soft light filtered through the trees onto Spanish tiles. After passing
the courtyard and fountain, my two friends and I slipped past the
old church and into the garden. Meandering paths surrounded by
roses and the occasional stone bench offered room to ponder and
explore. As we passed statues of saints and historical figures, we
found ourselves looking through the tall gates that enclosed the
garden, and we could see the bustling city spread in the valley below.

We didn't have to travel to Europe to find this jewel. Instead,
my friends in San Diego and I wanted to find a place to pray for
our city, and we decided to visit Mission Basilica San Diego de
Alcalá, the place where Christianity had first come to the West
Coast. This historical place was of great significance two hundred
years ago, when monks from Spain set up a mission to reach the
indigenous people with the gospel of Christ. One of them even
died as a martyr. During a violent raid, his final words were, "Love
God, my brothers."

This place was significant to the spiritual birth of Christianity
in our city, so we decided to take a "mini-pilgrimage" for an af-
ternoon to visit this site. We asked God to lead us, show us what
we needed to learn from this place, and make some time to pray
together for our city. When we left, we had a greater respect for
the price that was paid to bring the gospel to our region. We felt
more connected to that history and could pray more fervently as
a result. Feeling refreshed after spending time in a beautiful place,
we all felt richer for the experience. And we'd only had to travel
twenty minutes down the freeway to find our pilgrim destination.
That's something we can all do!

When considering the idea of a pilgrimage, you don't have to
leave your country or travel around the world. Chances are, there
are pilgrim sites all around you. With a little bit of research, you
can find Christian places of spiritual significance within a day trip
of where you live. Taking a trip by yourself or with a group can

be a great way to embrace this divine adventure. As a result, you can connect with the personal history of your region, spend time praying for your area, and have some special time with the Lord as you journey with him.

Planning a Pilgrimage

When planning a pilgrimage, here are a few things to consider. First, when you build your trip, allow yourself to dream about what it could look like, and think about what you want to accomplish while you're there. For instance, if you want to visit the Holy Land, ask yourself what kind of trip you'd like to go on. Do you want to learn about history, help a local church, or spend time in meditation and prayer at holy sites? (Many friends of mine have booked a trip to Israel and felt overwhelmed by a frantic schedule of tourist stops when they actually wanted more of a meditative experience. Make sure you ask yourself the right questions before you go so you can meet your goals.) Here are a few questions to help you start dreaming. Be honest with your answers. What makes you come alive?

- If I could go on an adventure with God to any destination in the world, where would it be?
- Would this require local or international travel?
- Would this trip be focused on prayer and spiritual enrichment?
- Do I see this trip as a chance to help others on the mission field?
- Am I interested in places of historical significance?
- Am I looking for solitude, or do I prefer social time with a group/team dynamic?
- Would I be willing to travel alone, or would I like to go with others?

- Do I see myself creating (blog, film, book, etc.) on this journey?
- What are the top three things I'd like to take away from this trip?
- How much time can I afford to take for travel?

Write or journal your responses and take them to prayer. Tell God your desire, and ask him to make a way, giving him liberty to change or tweak what you've written. Then start researching what a pilgrimage could look like. If you don't have the funds, just keep praying. If you want to travel overseas, one good step of faith is to purchase your passport and be ready to go. Things can happen quickly when God opens the door.

When taking your trip, make time to pray each morning, asking the Lord to protect and guide you by opening the doors, and be available to offer his love to others. Be prepared to listen to and learn and grow from the people you'll meet along the way as a modern-day pilgrim. Keep a daily journal if you can, because you'll have experiences to remember for the rest of your life. Your faith will grow and your heart will be richer when you return home. Have a great adventure!

Your Turn

- What are some benefits of taking a pilgrimage?
- Can you see yourself taking one?
- What would be your ultimate trip?
- Do you think God could be calling you to take a pilgrimage?

Spiritual Practice

Allow yourself to dream about taking a pilgrimage. Ask the Lord if he would like you to make plans to build a trip. While many people take trips to holy sites, take some time to consider what works for you and recognize that he is able to give a creative plan. Whether it's to a local site or a location around the world, your journey can be a lot of fun. Ask yourself if there's a church or ministry you'd enjoy visiting in person, and make plans to attend. Christian conferences and events can also act as a pilgrimage when you dedicate the trip to seeking the Lord at each step. Brainstorm an adventure, pray about it, and see what God will do!

SEVEN

Obedience

THE KEY TO PARTNERING WITH GOD

I'm not a dog person. I'm kind of allergic to pets, actually. The funny thing is that one of my favorite books is about a Canadian sheep dog. It stole my heart, and I decided that if I could be any animal, I'd definitely be at least part sheep dog. When I put all my belongings in storage and lived out of suitcases while traveling for a few years, I discovered that some of the only things I missed in my minimalist life were my top ten favorite books . . . including the sheep dog story. The reason I love that particular book is this: it helps me understand me. It offers a grid for my desire to be passionately devoted to something real . . . that's bigger than me . . . a destiny I was made for. Not just to be loved by God but to partner with him. It was a thought I couldn't put into words until this book about a frightened sheep dog and her kind master made that idea real.

The story is a small volume by Phillip Keller called *Lessons from a Sheep Dog: A True Story of Transforming Love*. It tells the true story of Lass, a mistreated and abused border collie. Even after she was bought by Phillip, a kind shepherd who recognized her potential to be an outstanding sheep dog, she was too terrified to be of any use to his herd. Her broad chest, intelligent eyes, and fascination with sheep were obvious signs of her natural instincts, but her calling was buried beneath layers of fear. A comfortable kennel was prepared for Lass, but she refused to eat and continued to growl at her master.

One day Phillip decided to turn her completely loose. Quick as lightning, Lass fled to the open fields, and he wondered if he'd seen the last of her. Then one day, Lass returned, responding in friendship to her master. Phillip writes,

> Suddenly I felt a soft warm nose touch my hands. Lass had come! My heart seemed to stop with ecstasy. Contact had been made! She had found the fortitude to let me touch her life. Lass discovered that she had a new master she could truly trust . . . who really loved her, who understood her, who had only her best interests in mind.
>
> She also began to realize that not only did I understand her, but I also knew all about sheep, ranching, and the exciting part she could play in the whole operation.[1]

Eventually Lass became the best sheep dog a shepherd could ask for, and she became a one-man dog, completely devoted to Phillip. She learned hand signals quickly and could gather the sheep from a long distance with just a wave of the shepherd's hand. They became a team, because the shepherd knew exactly what this beautiful dog was made for and he helped her become all she was made to be. Together, they kept the sheep safe, fed, and well cared for, and Lass thrived while working closely with the shepherd.

Phillip writes about how this experience taught him about his relationship with Christ: how Jesus redeems us from a life of fear, and he sees the calling and potential that's been wired into our lives by a loving Creator. The Good Shepherd knows that the only place we will thrive is walking and working closely with him. Just like Lass, when we listen to his voice, we experience deep fulfillment and joy. In order to get to that place, we have to fight a battle no one can wage for us: the determination to conquer our fears and learn the lessons of *trust and obedience*.

How God Wins Our Hearts

Lass's story resonates so much with me, because I know what it's like to stare into the face of fear and wonder if I can trust God enough to obey him. When my will and God's collide, often it's because I'm afraid . . . scared that what he is asking of me will lead to disaster. That I will step out to follow and be left alone . . . or that his commands will steal my enjoyment of life. Thankfully, we're talking about a God whose very name is *Faithful* and *True*. He has a proven track record and loves to respond to his children. The reward is a beautiful partnership between us and Jesus as we grow in the ability to hear and respond to his voice.

Repeatedly, the Scriptures relate the kind words of Jesus about the importance of obedience. Because God is passionate about our well-being, he knows what's best for us, and straying from his path can bring us so much grief. We're his children, and our pain brings him no pleasure, so when he calls us to obey, he's inviting us to build lives that are solid and strong and will withstand the trials that will come. If we don't obey him, we miss the opportunity to follow through with our faith. In Luke 6, Jesus laments,

> But why do you call Me "Lord, Lord," and not do the things which I say? Whoever comes to Me, and hears My sayings and does them, I will show you whom he is like: He is like a man building a house, who dug deep and laid the foundation on the rock. And when the flood arose, the stream beat vehemently against that house, and could not shake it, for it was founded on the rock.

But he who heard and did nothing is like a man who built a house on the earth without a foundation, against which the stream beat vehemently; and immediately it fell. And the ruin of that house was great.

vv. 46–49

During the Last Supper, some of Christ's final words to the disciples involved the call to obedience, wedged between his promises of partnership and help, and the foretelling of the Holy Spirit's companionship to help with his assignments. He longs to partner with us in the things that truly matter, so that our lives on earth will accomplish the most good, and we'll be investing in things of eternal value.

If you ask anything in My name, I will do it.

If you love Me, keep My commandments. And I will pray the Father, and He will give you another Helper, that He may abide with you forever—the Spirit of truth, whom the world cannot receive, because it neither sees Him nor knows Him; but you know Him, for He dwells with you and will be in you. I will not leave you orphans; I will come to you.

John 14:14–18

When our hearts are truly after God, we discover that his intentions are kind: he equips, listens, understands, and will never leave us alone. He's a good Father who has no orphans—he loves to help his children.

Why Obey?

In our humanness, it's easy to struggle with the *why* of obeying God. We're not born into this world knowing him, so we have to choose whether or not to follow his commands. One of the biggest opportunities humankind is offered is the chance to learn of his kindness and choose to trust and obey him.

When our hearts are truly
after God, we discover that
his intentions are kind:
he equips, listens,
understands, and will
never leave us alone.
He's a good Father
who has no orphans—
he loves to help his children.

Two scriptural examples of people who struggled with obedience are Pharaoh in the book of Exodus and the bride in Song of Solomon. Each of them had the opportunity to respond to a call. By unpacking these two scenarios, we'll discover why obedience matters so much.

Pharaoh's Choice

The air thickened with tension as Moses entered the palace and stood face-to-face with the king of Egypt. Pharaoh was not a man prone to mercy—he beat and tortured the Israelite slaves, considered them his personal property, and forced them to build stone cities without pay. Fearing a rebellion among the thousands of Hebrew slaves, the ruler's father had ordered all male babies to be slaughtered. This king neither feared God nor had any desire to change his ways.

Upon approaching the throne, Moses appealed for the end of slavery in the name of Yahweh, a God unknown to the idol-worshiping Egyptians: "Thus says the Lord God of Israel, 'Let my people go!'"

Pharaoh swiftly brushed off Moses's words. "Who is the Lord that I should obey his voice?" he responded from the lavish throne. "I do not know the Lord and have no intention of letting Israel go."

Moses leaned on his staff, urging the king to consider his words carefully; his face shone with clear determination as he challenged the king's words.

"The God of the Hebrews has met with us," he said confidently. "Please let us go three days' journey into the wilderness and worship the Lord our God."

With a cynical laugh, Pharaoh cryptically opted for a decree of his own.

"Let the slaves make bricks without straw," he commanded, knowing that the command would mean sleepless nights for the Israelites as they gathered stubble for use in their mortar. The royal meeting was over. Pharaoh couldn't care less about God's commands.

Grief-stricken, Moses left the palace and began to pray.

Pharaoh's heart is hard, the Lord told him, *he refuses to let the people go.*

Only then did God begin to give clear direction for the ten plagues to be released on Egypt, pausing in between each to see if the king's heart had changed. God was kind but firm; his people were meant to be free, and as long as they were enslaved, their taskmasters would only experience difficulty.[2]

Unfortunately, Pharaoh never got to the point of trusting God or obeying him. Even when he finally let the Israelites go, he changed his mind afterward, chasing them and causing the death of his entire nation's army when they drowned in the Red Sea as God defended his people.[3]

The whole story is a tragic tale that revolves around the question from Pharaoh, *Who is the Lord that I should obey him?* This Egyptian king never discovered the answer; he was too busy defending his pride and the ability to control his kingdom, which he eventually lost because he refused to put God first. If he had taken the time to discover that Yahweh was the one true God, Pharaoh and his entire kingdom could have been spared so much pain. This lack of obedience came at a very high price.

Our response to this question impacts the outcome of our lives too. When we choose to obey the Lord, we're acknowledging that he has the right to ask for our allegiance because he's the sovereign God of the universe. One way or another, he will have his way, and choosing to rebel against his commands means there's a high price to pay. Yet, if we come to know him, we'll discover that he's our biggest cheerleader, longing to work things for our good and keep us from trouble.

The true concept of obedience starts by asking, *Who is the Lord?* And as we learn who he is, it becomes the most logical thing in the world to obey his voice.

The Bride and the King

Another *why* question in Scripture is found in the middle of a love story. It's a fascinating picture of the struggles within obedience and the ultimate triumph of love.

A shepherdess has fallen in love with the king, and he has chosen her as his bride. Elated, she's madly in love with how wonderful he is! She can't stop talking about how amazing his attributes are, and she's ready to spend her life with this man.

One night, she hears her lover's knock at the door. She recognizes his voice and her heart leaps, but she's too tired to get up and let him in. Finally, feeling bad for not responding, she gets up to open the door . . . but it's too late. Only the lingering scent of his cologne remains. Heartbroken, she runs into the dark streets to find him. Song of Solomon records her words, as if written in a lover's journal:

> I opened for my beloved,
> But my beloved had turned away and was gone.
> My heart leaped up when he spoke.
> I sought him, but I could not find him;
> I called him, but he gave me no answer.
>
> Song of Solomon 5:6

Running into the chilly night air, the woman searches to find him, even asking her girlfriends and the watchmen of the city to help. We aren't told the exact moment of their meeting, but eventually the two lovers are reunited and their bond is restored. As they marvel at their beautiful relationship, the estrangement of the night slips away.

The book of Song of Solomon is often used to depict the love relationship between Christ and the church, and we can glean some insight on obeying Christ as we unpack these words in this light. Just like the bride of Christ, this woman is head over heels in love with the king because she's experienced his goodness. There's no need to talk her into the relationship—she's 100 percent on board with being his bride. Like many Christians, she's ready to be fully committed to a glorious relationship. Unlike Pharaoh, who had no knowledge of God or any intention to learn of him, this woman represents the believer who is excited and passionate about their relationship with Jesus.

On the other hand, the struggle with obedience is real, just as it is for many people who love Christ but wrestle with responding when he calls them to follow. When her lover calls her during the middle of the night, she's a bit more concerned about her comfort than about responding to his voice.

The king knocks but doesn't force his entrance, just as the Lord tugs on our hearts but never demands obedience. Instead, he waits to see how we'll respond to his voice, and it's our choice whether or not to open the door. God's call to obedience may come at an inconvenient moment. We may love the Lord and desire to be connected to him, but it can still be a struggle. *I'm too comfortable right now*, we might say. *Come back another time!* Yet, if we truly long for a close connection with Christ, we have to recognize that responding to his voice is crucial to our relationship with him.

> Her heart's desire
> was for the king's embrace.
>
> Yet in her disregard
> she did not heed his call
> to share her time with him.
>
> Her love was for the king
> and yet she did not
> own her love.

Just like the bride, we all miss the opportunity to hear and obey the call sometimes, but when we do, let's pursue Jesus until we get back on track. None of us follow Christ perfectly, but our Savior is always ready to reconnect with us when we search for him and refocus our hearts on the relationship. The communion is restored as we pursue him with passion again. Choosing to obey the call of Jesus is an important part of having a healthy relationship with him.

Choice to Follow

I remember the first time I heard the call to obedience in a way that challenged me to step out of my comfort zone. After making the choice to dedicate my heart to Christ as a child, I couldn't say that I actually sensed his presence or leading in my life. Reading stories of missionaries and people who had amazing experiences with God inspired me, so I began to pray that I would hear his voice speak to my heart too.

One day I was struggling with how a schoolmate was treating me in high school. Feeling rejected and wrestling with self-pity, I told God my troubles. Suddenly, I heard the Lord speak to me. It wasn't audible, but it may as well have been because the message was unmistakable.

At one point you said you wanted to follow me—do you still want to? If so, forgive them.

I was shocked. My heart was a bit torn. On one hand, I knew beyond a shadow of a doubt that God had spoken to me. The message was as clear as a bell. It was thrilling! Yet, just like the comfortable shepherdess, I knew he was asking me to do what I didn't feel like doing. I was feeling very justified in my sense of betrayal in an unfair situation, and I was hoping that God would defend my pride. Much to my chagrin, he challenged me to be like Jesus and show mercy instead.

Sometimes following Jesus is not the most comfortable option in life. The spiritual discipline of obedience will be polarizing at times, because God never promises to give us everything we want or to justify our pride. Instead, he gives us himself, and offers to make us like Jesus. Of what worth is our petty pride in comparison with the high calling of becoming like the Lord? If we want to follow Jesus more than anything else in the world, we'll make the right choice. It won't always be easy, but the price will be worth the reward of knowing and following him fully.

Practicing Obedience

So how do we practice obedience? Do we wait for God to send a lightning bolt from heaven, commanding us to obey? Here are a few practical ways we can follow, trusting that he will guide us as we listen for his voice.

- **Following the written Word:** If a topic is in God's Word, it usually is pretty obvious what he's leading us to do. Sexual morality, finances, the way we use our words, and how to treat others are all clearly mapped out in the Scriptures. It doesn't take a supernatural experience for us to know what God requires of us—just open the Book and find out!

- **Obeying the Holy Spirit:** Often, the voice of God speaks through motivating our conscience. His gentle nudge can give us a sense of peace or a "check in the spirit" about decisions we need to make. This is where prayer and sensitivity to his voice come into play as we ask the Lord to help us discern between our own emotions and the still, small voice of Jesus.

- **Personal direction:** When the apostle Paul was taking a missionary journey, he wanted to visit Asia and Bithynia yet was stopped both times by the Holy Spirit. Eventually he had a dream of a man from Macedonia saying, "Come over here and help us!" (Acts 16:6–10). Because of his consistency in waiting on God and obeying when called, the church in Philippi was born and we have the book of Philippians today. Sometimes the Holy Spirit might close a door, but if we simply pray and wait on him, we'll discover the right open one.

- **Relationships:** The Lord is a great relationship coach! I can't tell you how many times I've sensed the prompting to befriend someone or had moments when he's steered me away from investing in a relationship that wouldn't be right for me down the road. Sometimes he will give me just the right words to speak encouragement to a person. Or perhaps he'll prompt me to be silent when I want to speak words that would make *me* feel better but wouldn't really help the situation. If we invite him into our relationships, he is quick to respond with his promptings.

Like the bride who responded to the king's knock on her door, obedience is simply an invitation to deeper intimacy and closeness with Jesus. Just as Lass the sheep dog learned to trust the shepherd, the more we learn to respond to Christ, the more we'll partner with his work in our lives and in the world around us. The rewards of obedience are the essence of what most believers long for in their walk with Christ: a fruitful life with a tangible closeness to the Savior. Sometimes we can be our own worst enemy and sabotage this process, but if our hearts are soft toward Christ, we'll get back on track quickly and follow him out of a heart of love. The practice of obedience is an amazing key to the divine adventure of following Christ.

Your Turn

- When you think of obedience, do you see it as a joy or a struggle?
- How does the idea of partnership with Christ affect your view?

- Why is obedience important?
- Is there an area of your life where God is tugging on your heart in regard to obedience?
- What would you say to someone else who is struggling to obey God?

Spiritual Practice

When you spend time with God in prayer, take some time to ask if there is an area of your life in which he wants to partner with you as you step out and obey. Take your time and listen for his response. Sometimes he may show you an area of purity that he wants you to embrace, a relationship to let go of, or a person he wants you to reach out to. The answer may come in the next few days when God brings a situation across your path and nudges you to respond to his prompting. Get ready for the adventure of partnering with the Lord as you follow his leading!

EIGHT

Meekness

FORGING HIDDEN STRENGTH

Outside my window, the colorful streets of Jerusalem buzzed with action. The calls of shop owners, aroma of fresh bagels, and parade of black-clad priests with swinging lamps of incense created an ever-changing motif in the streets. While filming a television show, I'd booked a room in a guesthouse and was looking forward to some time off to see the sights. Passover was approaching, and I reveled in the prospect of experiencing the season from the city where Jesus had shared this holy day with his disciples thousands of years ago.

With classic American zeal, I bounced up to the front desk. "I'd like to confirm my place in the Passover service and meal this Thursday night," I said to the clerk in the starched white shirt. She checked her notes, scanning the list of attendees with an aura of importance.

"Sorry, you are not on the list."

My eyes widened in dismay as I quickly, and a little sharply, responded, "But I emailed before arriving. The staff told me to let you know I am to be included when I checked in."

"We were not informed," she responded crisply. "I'll let you know if any openings come available."

My heart sank. I had booked my trip to Israel specifically to include a Passover service, with both a meal and liturgy, celebrating the Last Supper just like Jesus had with his twelve disciples, and this was to be a highlight of the trip.

"Could I just sit in a corner and watch?" I asked, pleading for a way in. "I don't have to eat the meal . . . I just want to enjoy the experience."

"We'll have to ask the man who is leading the service," she responded, slightly defensively. In her mind, the conversation was obviously over.

Disappointment flooded my thoughts, threatening to overturn my excitement of the day. I wanted to fight back. To show her my emails and demand attention from the manager. To threaten to write terrible reviews online if I didn't get my way. I felt cheated! The angst of the moment threatened to ruin my day. But since I was planning to stay at this location for a number of days, I didn't want to make a scene that would affect the rest of my trip. In my heart, I knew that the best thing I could do was to remain polite and take the situation to God.

I slipped back to my room and got on my knees. "Lord," I said, making my case before God, "you know how deeply I looked forward to this. Would you please send a remedy?"

Over the next few days, I simply prayed, knowing it would take a miracle to move my name up the list. One morning, I sensed a simple prompting from the Lord: *Go to the chapel and worship.*

There was no one in the arched chapel room when I stepped inside. I'd already been granted permission to play the baby grand piano that the community used for worship services, so I slid back

Sounds of piano, voice,

and melodious flute filled

the ancient room. It was

an incredible moment

of divine adventure . . .

worshiping with a stranger

in an Israeli chapel.

the black lid and placed my fingers on the keys. Letting my heart soar in song, I played with all my might and worshiped the Lord.

Soon, a Middle Eastern man entered the back of the sanctuary. He surveyed the scene and then slipped out the door. I ignored the unexpected guest and continued worshiping. A few minutes later he returned with a silver flute. Walking up to the piano, he began to play along. Sounds of piano, voice, and melodious flute filled the ancient room. It was an incredible moment of divine adventure . . . worshiping with a stranger in an Israeli chapel.

After we played several songs, he formally introduced himself as Ethan, a worker at the guesthouse. He was delighted to meet another worshiper of Christ, and we became fast friends.

Later that day I checked back with the front desk about the Passover service. I decided to take the humble approach, shooting up a prayer before mustering my courage to approach them.

Lord, I prayed silently, *I don't need the feast. I just want to enjoy this special moment during Passover in Jerusalem with you.*

I took a deep breath and approached the brusque clerk.

"Is there a way I could attend the service . . . maybe just sit in a corner in the back of the room? I don't need any food. I'd just like to worship in silence."

"Well," the desk clerk responded, "we'll have to ask Ethan."

Ethan? I thought. *That's a curious coincidence . . . I've just met a man by that name.*

By some divine strategy, it was the same person! And since we had just struck up a friendship, he immediately invited me to join the service. On the evening of Passover, Ethan pulled up an extra chair to his right-hand side and asked me to sit next to him and assist him in leading the service. I received special treatment *at the head of the table*!

The food was terrific . . . I didn't have to settle for crumbs or a seat in the corner, although I would have gladly done so. Not only had God made a way for me to join the service but I'd been promoted from the bottom of the list to sitting with the leader.

All this had happened without having to threaten or argue with the clerk. But I *could* have held on to my anger, staying frustrated with the system and allowing my temper to get the better of me. Instead, I decided to practice the spiritual discipline of meekness: to take the lowest place and pray. In his creativity, God didn't change the system or cause someone to give me their seat. He had another plan. I found myself promoted to the head of the table, enjoying the feast with a new friend.

Discovering Meekness

Even as children, we're trained to compete for the best seats or be left out of the game. The game Musical Chairs has taught us to listen closely while a tune plays—and then run when it stops, feverishly pushing others out of the way until we secure our place in the circle. We know what happens when we are too slow. We're out of the game, ashamedly sitting on the sidelines until we're given another chance. Slowing down means failure. We vow to get ahead next time—to be better. We'll push harder to win.

The spiritual practice of meekness counters the frantic momentum of "the game" with quiet dignity. It realizes there's more at stake than winning. So, it pauses instead of racing ahead. It checks its tongue and holds it when needed. It chooses its fights carefully, often on the battlefield of prayer where only God sees. And he rewards.

When practicing meekness, we realize that sometimes we don't have to make it all happen, because Another is ready to fight for us. Instead of us bowing to the rhythms of this world, the Lord wants to be the music we listen for. The One who reserves our seat at the table. Or makes a new one. He loves calling us from obscurity to prominence. Far from a cowardly trait, meekness places the disciple on the fast track to experiencing God's divine adventure.

Jesus told a story of meekness and humility that also involved seats at a table. While being hosted in the home of a Pharisee, he

When practicing meekness,

we realize that sometimes

we don't have to make

it all happen, because

Another is ready

to fight for us.

noticed how quickly the guests chose the honored seats for themselves. It was Musical Chairs in the first century . . . to see who could quickly secure the closest place to Jesus, the guest of honor.

> So He told a parable to those who were invited, when He noted how they chose the best places, saying to them: "When you are invited by anyone to a wedding feast, do not sit down in the best place, lest one more honorable than you be invited by him; and he who invited you and him come and say to you, 'Give place to this man,' and then you begin with shame to take the lowest place. But when you are invited, go and sit down in the lowest place, so that when he who invited you comes he may say to you, 'Friend, go up higher.' Then you will have glory in the presence of those who sit at the table with you. For whoever exalts himself will be humbled, and he who humbles himself will be exalted."
>
> Luke 14:7–11

Jesus didn't buy into the game. Instead of patting the shoulders of the guests who vied for the seats of honor, he actually commended those who took the lowest seat at the table. He did not do so to applaud displays of martyrdom or self-deprivation. *Instead, he demonstrated a desire to promote his friends.* Embracing humility and meekness gives God space to work on our behalf. It's choosing the low place and waiting for him to move. It's hard. And good. A key to unlocking our divine adventure with the King.

Redefining Meekness

Jesus didn't just teach people *about* meekness; *he lived it.* He knew the angst of turning down a good thing in favor of something greater, even when the "greater" didn't look like much in the moment.

Instead of coming with a blaze of glory that revealed the magnificent power of God to humankind, he came in disguise. Clothed in flesh. In a stable. Meek and lowly. When offered an earthly throne, he chose a cross. He beat the world's game, but not by their rules. The King of Heaven bowed down low and touched earth, demonstrating a life that moves to the music of heaven.

> Though he was God,
>> he did not think of equality with God
>> as something to cling to.
> Instead, he gave up his divine privileges;
>> he took the humble position of a slave
>> and was born as a human being.
> When he appeared in human form,
>> he humbled himself in obedience to God
>> and died a criminal's death on a cross.
>
> Therefore, God elevated him to the place of highest honor
>> and gave him the name above all other names,
> that at the name of Jesus every knee should bow,
>> in heaven and on earth and under the earth,
> and every tongue declare that Jesus Christ is Lord,
>> to the glory of God the Father.
>
> Philippians 2:6–11 NLT

Even in his bold lifestyle, Christ showed us what meekness means. While unafraid to stand up for justice by giving strong, challenging words to the Pharisees, even making a whip to overturn the tables of the greedy money changers in the temple, he also was deeply caring and compassionate, using a basin and towel to wash his disciples' feet. He was unyielding in principles of purity and matters of truth, yet we see a soft side to his nature that takes away any fear of approaching him.

Meekness is the gentle side of Jesus. Here are a few ways we see it:

- Little children came to the Lord, and when the apostles tried to spare him the trouble of listening to them, he rebuked them. Gathering the little ones around him, he

134

placed his hands on them and spoke words of blessing (Matt. 19:13–15).

- He wept over the city of Jerusalem and longed to protect it like a hen does her chicks (Matt. 23:37).
- When Jesus met Mary and Martha after their brother died, he wept along with them, even while knowing that he was about to raise Lazarus from the dead (John 11:35).
- The apostle John, probably a teenager when first following Christ, laid his head on the Lord during the Last Supper (John 13:23).

Velvet-Covered Steel

Like Jesus, you don't have to be a weak person in order to practice meekness. Quite the opposite: meekness shines brightly in the lives of those who stand for what's important, but they choose to wield their words and actions in ways that make them approachable to others.

One such man was President Abraham Lincoln, of whom poet and biographer Carl Sandburg wrote, "Not often in the story of mankind does a man arrive on earth who is both steel and velvet, . . . who holds in his heart and mind the paradox of terrible storm and peace unspeakable and perfect."[1]

The idea of velvet-covered steel deftly paints a colorful picture of a person robed in meekness: one who carries a strong backbone of moral character yet is gentle and approachable when needed. One fascinating story of President Lincoln typifies this idea of meekness, even when under tremendous pressure.

During the Civil War, Lincoln spent many hours listening to mothers, fathers, and wives of soldiers who were caught in the bloody War Between the States. Desertion was punishable by death, so many family members came to plead for a soldier's life if circumstances required him to leave the front lines. One account tells of a fifteen-year-old boy named John Bullock who came to the president requesting parole for his dying brother, a Confederate soldier.

Lincoln could have ignored this Southern boy's request, refusing him mercy because he was on the "other side" of the war. The brother had possibly killed some of Lincoln's own men. Honest Abe hated the shedding of blood . . . despised the terrible gruesomeness of this war . . . yet in the middle of the pressure, he chose to extend mercy. Instead of acting out of vengeance, Lincoln personally signed the order of release and treated the boy with kindness. Later, the teenager wrote,

> Before approaching the President I felt a natural diffidence, not to say awe, of the man who was Chief Executive of the nation, commander-in-chief of the army and navy, as well as the man who held the life of my brother in his keeping.
>
> To a boy of fifteen this feeling was only natural. The closer I approached the great man, however, the less I feared him, the higher my courage rose; and before the interview was over I was as much at my ease with President Lincoln as if talking to my own father.
>
> The reasons for this are to be found in just the qualities of heart with which he is accredited, and rightly so, by all the world. No sooner had he laid his hand upon my shoulder and said, "My son," than I felt drawn to him, and dreaded less and less the interview he had granted me; and each successive question he asked me put me more at my ease, until, when I was alone with him in his private office, all my embarrassment vanished, and I saw before me the countenance of a man I could trust, one which invited confidence.[2]

The fact that a teenager could feel so comfortable with the president while requesting mercy for a dying Confederate soldier reveals so much of the "velvet" represented in Lincoln's life. He fought a war for the sake of justice, but his heart was never hardened by the polarizing nature of the cause. His stance was a gentle, caring response toward hurting soldiers *on both sides*. Meekness was not unbecoming to his position.

Not only did Lincoln win the war, but his position of compassion in the face of pressure enabled steps to be taken toward rebuilding the nation after the terrible rift between the North and South.[3] Meekness didn't suppress his influence: it broadened it. This is exactly what Scripture reveals in the true meaning of meekness: *strength clothed in gentleness, like velvet-covered steel.*

Socially Meek

While many people would paint meekness with soft brushes in dull, muted colors, I believe the authentic definition requires bold blues and yellows. It requires a palette knife with an edge. It takes grit. Only the brave and undaunted have the courage to display this trait that heaven loves to honor. God even promises a special type of beauty for those who embrace this trait.

> For the LORD taketh pleasure in his people:
> he will beautify the meek with salvation.
>
> Psalm 149:4 KJV

One of the best places to practice meekness is on social media: an open, and sometimes polarizing, forum of thought in our modern world. Whether it's a smiling cat, a new political perspective, or what someone ate for lunch, most topics are fair game, right? It reminds me of Athens in the first century, the great center of philosophy and open thought at the time. The book of Acts describes the Athenians this way:

> For all the Athenians and strangers which were there spent their time in nothing else, but either to tell, or to hear some new thing.
>
> Acts 17:21 KJV

Doesn't that perfectly describe social media today?! Everyone has a voice, and many have no qualms about using it to post their current mood swing. Personally, I enjoy social media. It's a great way to create community and connect with people around the world. However, it's easy to wage a war of words toward views we disagree with. Unless we embrace meekness, social media is simply another way to carelessly voice an opinion and not care about how it impacts others. Practicing the spiritual discipline of meekness means that we speak truth with boldness, clearly standing for justice, while also responding with humility and gentleness. We don't lash out at others, get defensive when someone challenges us (I'm still working on this one), or make unreasonable accusations. We let our light shine brightly, but we don't have to speak disrespectfully to others while doing so.

I have a tendency to have pretty strong opinions, and social media is just the thing to push my buttons. Maybe you know the feeling . . . you're scrolling through a news feed on your phone during a spare moment in the day and a post catches your attention. *What?!* Flicking your thumb over an image, you click to read the whole post . . . interest piqued . . . eyes widening . . . your blood pressure starts to rise. *I can't believe it. How could they post such a thing! They should know better.* You immediately start to respond, trying to talk some sense into your media friend. Or acquaintance. Or a stranger who randomly followed you because your second cousin did. The injustice of the moment has pulled you in like a moth to the flame.

I'll be honest: there are times I've been so impassioned when responding to a post or message that I've lost a friend. Not just a distant friend but a good friend. With the sting of regret, I've realized it's easy to respond without thinking my answer through. Practicing meekness in these moments is one thing I've chosen to learn because I want to be intentional about how to both express my passion and communicate it well. Here are a few things I've learned:

- First, I take some time to reread the post and make sure I'm fully understanding the text and not just triggered by something I assumed was said.

- Often, I pray, asking God for wisdom and pausing to sort through my emotion if it's aimed toward someone I care about. I ask God if he wants me to speak or just to pray and commit the situation to him.
- Next, I consider whether to send a private message to the person, especially if they're a personal friend. I don't want to embarrass them by disagreeing with their statement online, but I will challenge them in graciousness if it's someone I think would care to listen to a differing view.
- I use clear communication when posting, not leaving room for points to be vague or easily misunderstood. And I try to end with a positive sentence. This helps the reader not to feel accused or attacked even though I have a differing opinion.

These tips apply when communicating not only in a vague relationship on social media but also in real life. When a friend or family member says something that's difficult or even hurtful, we can choose to respond with meekness rather than frustration. How easy it is to play a game of Musical Chairs within a conversation! We vie for the open space, trying to beat each other with wit and arguments instead of inviting God in, pausing to listen for his music, and living by the rhythm. Sometimes that means taking the lowest place, even when it's not what we would normally do.

> Meekness
> shines brightest,
> not in weakness
> but in strength.
>
> Those who live
> with strength of passion
> may find meekness
> a challenge to embrace,
> and yet they wear it
> in his strength most nobly.

Those who wisely govern
their own hearts
entrust themselves to God.

They say,
I could, but I won't.
I won't control,
manipulate
or dominate
the situation.
I choose obedience to God
and wait on him
and trust in him,
believe in him
to move
on my behalf.

Practicing the spiritual discipline of meekness doesn't necessarily mean we avoid conflict or a difference of opinion but that we refuse to respond with defensiveness or self-protection in the heat of the battle. It's not always easy, but it's worth it. Not only do we start to look more like Christ, but we see his goodness show up right here in our world. Jesus invited us into a divine adventure when he said the words

Blessed are the meek,
For they shall inherit the earth.

Matthew 5:5

Your Turn

- What's your personal definition of *meekness*? Take a moment to journal your answer.
- How does this idea play out in your everyday life?

- Are there specific situations or relationships that require an extra measure of meekness?
- How do you think Christ would respond to these situations? Spend some time in prayer over this.

Spiritual Practice

Take a pen and paper into your quiet place of prayer. Ask the Holy Spirit to bring to mind a few ways that you can implement meekness in your life, and write them down. Perhaps there's a person at work, at home, on social media, or in your extended family who often rubs you the wrong way and causes your blood pressure to rise a bit.[4] Write down the person's name and spend some time praying for them. Then ask the Lord to show you how to respond with a gracious attitude, inviting him into the situation and asking him to move.

NINE

Sacred Rest

AN INVITATION TO INTIMACY

Okay, I'll admit it: resting is hard for me! When given the option of playing the game or sitting on the bench, I'll run to the field every time. I love putting feet to my faith and serving others, so when the time comes to rest, it's often harder than it should be. I'm a bit like the Energizer Bunny . . . on steroids. I pour my energy into projects, sometimes even driving myself to exhaustion, simply because I'm so excited for the outcome. Whether we find rest difficult or easy, we'll discover that being a follower of Christ enables us to weave meaningful rest into our lives in beautiful ways.

Learning how to intentionally rest well is a spiritual practice that helps us reset our bodies, hearts, and minds, but sometimes it's harder than we like to admit. However, the discipline of rest has life-giving, healing results. Recently I came across an article that offered a few benefits of physical rest, including that it

1. protects your heart from high blood pressure;
2. boosts your memory;

3. lowers your risk of a stroke;

4. keeps you safe from depression;

5. helps you make better decisions;

6. keeps you slim;

7. eases acne;

8. lowers your risk of catching a cold.[1]

That's a great list of perks. We thrive when we rest, yet life has a way of talking us out of this healing practice. Maybe you've wrestled with some of the excuses I have: *I feel lazy and unproductive when I rest. I get bored. I feel guilty for not being useful. There are so many people who need me, and I don't like to tell them no. Maybe I just enjoy being busy.* Or, maybe rest comes easy for you, and going to work is a little harder! Either way, God created a rhythm of rest and work by setting an example: after creating the world in six days, he rested on the seventh.

> On the seventh day God had finished his work of creation, so he rested from all his work. And God blessed the seventh day and declared it holy, because it was the day when he rested from all his work of creation.
>
> Genesis 2:2–3 NLT

After six days of making beautiful things, God stepped away from the process. In the Hebrew language, this word *rest* is *Sabbath*, meaning "repose, desist from exertion, celebrate." More than just taking a break from work, it was a holy space, a spiritual time set apart for a special purpose. It wasn't that the business of creating was bad or not enjoyable, but he set aside time to *celebrate what had been accomplished and rest.*

> Sometimes we need
> to back away
> from all the things
> that went before

to rest
rejoice
and celebrate—
just as God demonstrates.

Saying Yes to Rest

Many Jewish people still practice a day of Sabbath as a reminder of how God rested. If you visit Israel on a Saturday, the nation virtually shuts down for twenty-four hours, from Friday night through Saturday evening, and you may even be hard-pressed to find a gas station that's open. Rest is part of the weekly worship, and it's even mentioned in the Ten Commandments.

> Remember the Sabbath day, to keep it holy. Six days you shall labor and do all your work, but the seventh day is the Sabbath of the LORD your God. In it you shall do no work: you, nor your son, nor your daughter, nor your male servant, nor your female servant, nor your cattle, nor your stranger who is within your gates. For in six days the LORD made the heavens and the earth, the sea, and all that is in them, and rested the seventh day. Therefore the LORD blessed the Sabbath day and hallowed it.
>
> Exodus 20:8–11

Interestingly, this practice has affected the entire world through-out history. When God first gave the weekly command to rest, the idea was revolutionary. Everyone worked hard seven days a week, and only the rich could afford the luxury of resting. For over four hundred years, the nation of Israel had been enslaved in Egypt, and slaves *never* rested. Each man's life depended on his labor, and they were enslaved to their work by merciless taskmasters. If they didn't work, the result could be death, because slavery demanded constant, rigorous labor.

When God freed the nation of Israel, the idea of rest was com-pletely new—they were being treated like royalty! No longer were

145

they bound to serve cruel masters who demeaned them with forced labor. Instead, they were allowed and even *commanded* to rest by a God of love who valued and cared about their lives.

This presented a different way of thinking: God's people were challenged to rest for one day a week. Rest was an act of worship. It helped them shift their focus from striving for survival by their own efforts toward God's loving provision.

God valued his people, since even the poorest were granted the luxury of time off from their daily labor. Saying yes to rest was a way of valuing themselves and enjoying the benefits of serving God instead of being enslaved. In the same way, when we choose to rest, we're demonstrating that we're not "slaves to our work" but that we trust God to meet our needs. We work hard and give him our best, but we also recognize that he values us and promises to meet our needs.

Slaves No More

To tell the truth, I'm my own worst taskmaster sometimes. And sometimes that's a good thing. When I'm producing a film or writing a book, there are times that require pushing myself hard to get projects done. I remember a week in Alaska when I spent eighteen hours a day hiking mountains to shoot on location, rewriting the script, washing wet costumes for the next day, leading my team in devotionals, and filming behind the camera. I've spent several months at a time locked away, editing raw footage, where the monotony of film production is enough to drive a creative person completely stir-crazy. Obviously, if you're passionate about making your vision happen, then you'll push yourself to give your best to the project.

Yet, it's not effort alone that accomplishes the goal; it's the grace and goodness of God. One way to focus back on the Lord is by making deliberate time to rest during or between busy seasons. If I don't do this, I become a slave to my work, driven by the need to achieve. By resting, I'm shifting my heart toward God by saying, *Lord, I believe you are working alongside me in this project. Lives will be changed because of your grace, not just my good intentions. Even in the busyness, I trust you enough to rest.*

When we choose to rest, sometimes there's a mental wrestling match between what God says about rest and some of the lies that attempt to bind us to that slave mentality. Every now and then, I still have to challenge them with the truth, pointing my soul back to what I know God says about rest.

Lie: I have to constantly work to make things happen.

Truth: I will work hard but choose times of rest, trusting that God will provide.

Lie: Work defines my value: if I can get things done for myself or my family, I'll earn my worth or value.

Truth: In reality, Jesus fought for our value when he went to the cross. Our good intentions can't define our worth, because he did it fully.

Lie: Rest is boring and unproductive.

Truth: Rest is a means to be intimate with the Lord and celebrate his goodness. It's important for my health and our relationship.

God greatly values hard work, but if we don't rest, our thoughts tend toward slavery rather than the value and freedom of being his children. When we practice rest as a spiritual discipline, our faith grows as we cultivate intimacy with Christ and actively trust him in big and small ways.

Resting 101

One of the other challenges to resting is that it can be hard to rest in a way that really brings deep rejuvenation. Sure, it's easy

By resting, I'm shifting my heart toward God by saying, *Lord, I believe you are working alongside me in this project. Lives will be changed because of your grace, not just my good intentions. Even in the busyness, I trust you enough to rest.*

to watch a movie, schedule a spa session, or go for a walk, but finding things that truly rejuvenate the soul is sometimes easier said than done. Sometimes we need to redefine rest and apply it to our unique space. I found a tip for personalizing rest in a ski resort town in the Eastern Sierra mountains of California . . .

Huge pine trees lined the road to Mammoth Lakes, and with every bend, epic vistas and layers of mountain peaks met my eyes. Snowy peaks offered perfect powder for skiing, snowshoeing, and sledding, and this small town was a hot spot to tourists all year long. I had visited my friend Lauren several times here, and our days were filled with hiking to hot springs, canoeing with friends, and paddleboarding on mountain lakes.

One day we were curled up in a cozy lodge with darling cups of hot tea, chatting about God moments that shaped our lives.

"I had to learn how to rest," Lauren began. "I had just graduated from college, and I threw myself into ministry and volunteer work—my life was going a hundred miles an hour. Suddenly I hit a wall and realized I was completely burnt out. I had no grid for the definition of rest."

Lauren decided to experiment with the concept of rest, using ideas that seemed like obvious ways to recover her spiritual momentum. First, she read her Bible all day. But even though she loved God's Word, she didn't feel rested by the end of the day. Next, she pulled out her old journals in hopes of reading old entries and tracing a pattern of where God was moving in her life, but that practice only created more inner turmoil as she ended the day with no answers.

"Finally," she shared, "I walked down the street to the beach. There were very few people on the shore during the day, and I started skipping and dancing on the white sand. Dipping my toes in the foamy waves, twirling, and worshiping God like a little girl, my heart felt carefree as I enjoyed the Creator in his creation. I suddenly realized I felt so refreshed!

"I sensed God whisper to my heart. 'You get it, Lauren,' he said. 'Rest is doing what you love with me.'

"It was such a precious moment with God. I realized I could even do something that exerted a lot of energy, like running a marathon, and I could still be at rest as long as I was doing it with him."

I marveled at the simplicity of her statement: practicing spiritual rest can be as easy as finding what you love and bringing Christ into it. Our joy is refueled and our souls are restored when we discover what we enjoy and do it with our Father.

> Rest is an invitation to . . .
>
> Pause
> From our labor
>
> Spend time
> With our Friend
>
> Enjoy life
> With him.

Our divine adventure invites us to rest with Christ. It's not all about what we can accomplish *for* God but also how we choose to *be with him*. As we explore how to rest well with him, we'll discover that he is close by, ready to enjoy this practice with us.

A Deeper Rest

The spiritual practice of rest doesn't always happen on a beautiful beach or mountaintop. God meets us with rest in the ordinary days, when it's least expected and most needed. When there are too many dirty dishes. Or when pressures in work and relationships seem out of control. In the middle of messy situations, when the flurry of anxious thoughts arises, it's easy to spend energy trying to make it all work. We feel overwhelmed. Or small. Or overcommitted. Or alone. Our souls become weary, like a frantic hamster who can't quite figure out how to get off the wheel. Then the Father speaks:

> *Just rest.*
> *I've got this.*
> *I've got you.*
>
> *I'll do the work.*
> *Just rest.*
> *Trust me.*

One day I experienced God's call to practice rest in the funniest of ways . . .

Miles of Arizona highway stretched in front of my little car, marked with cacti and red rock, as I drove to speak at a small church. I'd never been to this place before, but my pastor friends had recommended it, and the church had booked me to speak at their Sunday service. Now, driving through the arid, desert mountains, I felt a little shiver of fear interrupt my thoughts. *If my car broke down on this road*, I thought, *I could be stuck out here for a long time.* Flipping on the radio, I hoped for a Christian music station that could help me think more positively, but the only signal my car could pick up was airing pop songs. At that moment, God used the cheeky lyrics from dance-rock band Walk the Moon's track to catch my attention: "Oh don't you dare look back. Just keep your eyes on me. . . . Shut up and dance with me."[2]

In the lyrics, the singer describes his longing to be with his girlfriend and how his thoughts were running wild. She simply pulls him onto the dance floor, encouraging him to focus on the relationship and embrace the moment.

I laughed out loud in the car. With panicking thoughts rivaling for my attention, I sensed the Holy Spirit saying, *Quiet your mind . . . dance with me. Trust that I will lead you through the desert.* Within a short time I arrived safely at the church, and the weekend

Our divine adventure
invites us to rest with Christ.
It's not all about what
we can accomplish *for* God
but also how we choose
to *be with him.*

ended up being a special time of ministry. Now every time I hear that pop song, I'm reminded to rest in the Lord!

This Scripture beautifully illustrates the idea of practicing rest in our daily lives:

> Rest in the LORD, and wait patiently for Him;
> Do not fret because of him who prospers in his way,
> Because of the man who brings wicked schemes to pass.
>
> Psalm 37:7

Unpacking the Hebrew words within this verse, we discover that *rest* means

to stop,

be silent,

quiet self,

rest,

to still,

tarry,

wait.

Part of intentionally resting in Christ means to quiet the chatter in our minds. To place a finger over our mouths when we start to panic or lose our peace. When our thoughts run wild, we can rest by taking a deep breath and choosing to be still. The words *wait patiently* are actually a single word in the Hebrew language that includes the meaning

to twist or whirl

in a circular manner,

to dance.

To rest and wait patiently for the Lord means to quiet our hearts and fully focus on him, trusting him to lead us through each step of life's journey like a lover in a dance. Even while moving we rest. We shift our focus from trying to get all the steps right to leaning on the shoulder of Christ. Our spiritual lives become a dance, allowing the lover of our soul to guide us as we rest in him.

Permission Granted to Rest

I encourage you to *give yourself permission to rest*! Sometimes we need to look ourselves in the mirror, lock eyes with our reflection, and tell ourselves, *You have the right to rest, and I am giving it to you.* God says your life is worth rest, and you can too.

If you need a little more encouragement, here are a few Scriptures that show how much God values rest:

- When Moses was leading the nation of Israel out of Egypt, they were led by a cloud of God's presence. When the cloud moved, they moved, and when it stopped, it was for a time of rest. God specifically moved at a pace that allowed for times of rest (Num. 9:18).
- God even commanded times for the land to rest every seventh year, knowing that overworked land would not yield a good harvest (Lev. 25:4–7).
- Jesus promises to give us rest (Matt. 11:28–30).
- Renewed strength is given to those who wait on him (Isa. 40:29).
- He gives sleep to those he loves (Ps. 127:2).
- He promises to be with us and give us rest (Exod. 33:14).

Scripture presents an amazing model of how God desires to rest with us. This doesn't mean that we stop working altogether, but our work becomes more meaningful as we practice times of refreshment and rest, and we can do it with him! Our divine adventure with Christ can include beautiful moments of rest.

Your Turn

- How well do you do with resting?
- Do you practice it often, or do you need to cultivate it more?
- What does a restful day look like to you?
- Are there some ways you can celebrate God's goodness when you rest?
- Like Lauren showed us, are there any ways you can "rest with God"?

Spiritual Practice

Schedule some time to rest with God. Get creative! Allow yourself to dream about what you enjoy doing rather than something that needs doing. Give your soul space to breathe. Then bring God into that time. Maybe you love soaking in a hot tub . . . find some waterproof earbuds and listen to your favorite worship music while you do! Or throw a quilt in a grassy park or your backyard and read a good book that refreshes you. Bring God with you when you rest, and you'll find it's just another way to deepen your relationship with him.

TEN

Giving

MAKE READY THE HARVEST

The tale of one man's generosity a thousand years ago was so legendary that it survived the ages and was crafted into a popular Christmas song.

Václav, duke of Bohemia, was born in AD 911 to a father who followed the Christian faith and a mother who was the daughter of a pagan tribal chief. Tragically, Václav's father died when the boy was only thirteen, and when his mother took the throne, she turned back to her pagan faith, murdering his Christian grandmother, who was mentoring Václav, and lashing out at other followers of Christ. For several years, Christianity underwent much persecution, until the young prince turned eighteen and took back the kingdom with the help of Christian nobles who still remained. He ruled with mercy and justice, defending his people and bringing German missionaries to offer fresh teaching about Christianity.[1]

One curious legend tells how Václav often rose in the middle of the night, leaving the castle to walk barefoot through the streets with only one chamberlain, giving generously to churches to help widows, orphans, and prisoners. Even though he only lived to the age of twenty-four, it is said that his devoted subjects considered him not just a ruler but the father of all afflicted people. Later, he was made a saint and given a title.[2]

We know this man as "Good King Wenceslas" from the popular Christmas carol. Folklore states that if the Czech people are ever in danger, an army of knights led by Wenceslas will rise from the Blaník mountain to defend them. St. Stephen's Day, December 26, is often a day when Václav is remembered, which is why we often sing of him at Christmastime, the season of giving.[3]

Throughout the ages, heroes of the Christian faith have been marked by the heartwarming attribute of generosity. Whether it's walking barefoot through the streets to give to the needy or building hospitals and clinics named for Christ and his followers, they've been known to go to great lengths to show kindness. Giving generously is one of the core values of the Christian faith, and this spiritual practice takes us farther down the path into our divine adventure.

A Father Who Gives

Everyone loves receiving gifts, especially if the giver knows exactly what we've always wanted! Some of my most precious memories are of shopping trips I took with my dad. When I visited him from out of town, he would take me to my favorite stores to get me a special gift. Sometimes he'd bless me a little more than I even felt comfortable receiving, and I'd say, "Oh Dad, you're spoiling me!"

"Rebecca," he'd admonish me in the gentlest of tones, "you're worth it! How often do I get the chance to bless you?"

Those words often brought a lump to my throat and tears to my eyes as I realized how much my dad loved his daughter. In that sweet way, he gave me a picture of the heart of my Father in heaven toward me: God is a giver, and he loves to give gifts to his

Giving generously is one of the core values of the Christian faith, and this spiritual practice takes us farther down the path into our divine adventure.

children. He doesn't give out of compulsion but simply because he is good and loves his kids. Because human beings are made in his image, even people who don't know God represent this love when they naturally want the best for their children. Parents who give gifts to their kids relish seeing the joy of their child's response! Scripture says,

> If you then, being evil, know how to give good gifts to your children, how much more will your Father who is in heaven give good things to those who ask Him!
>
> Matthew 7:11

When you become a Christian, you meet the Giver who out-gives everyone: our Father God. He has already given us so many things! In the beginning of creation, he gave us life and breath. Then he gave us the Scriptures to show us the way to live, and he offers provision, protection, and many other promises when we ask. Most of all, he gave the most precious gift in his Son, Jesus, to shed his own blood and purchase us back to God. Yet he didn't stop there! He then gave us the Holy Spirit as our Comforter and Guide and promises never to leave or forsake us. He is the God who keeps on giving!

As followers of Christ, one reason we practice giving is because we serve a generous God and we desire to reflect that goodness we've received. Like him, we don't give out of obligation but because we have the opportunity to reflect the image of the One we follow. This is the first reason for giving to others: because God is a giver, and we have the opportunity to be like him. As we imitate Christ, we learn to become a mirror image of him.

Receiving the Gift

When I was thirteen years old, someone gave me a gift that deeply impacted my bouncing, junior-high heart and challenged me to think about the power of generosity. When visiting a Colorado wilderness camp with my family, I was ecstatic to learn of free horseback rides. Mind you, horses were my obsession. Any horse movie available was watched over and over again in our home! I spent afternoons at my neighbors' stable, brushing their bay and gray Arabians, dreaming of the day that one of these noble beasts could be mine.

So when I discovered that the camp was hosting a horseback riding trip that lasted an *entire day*, I was elated! The only catch was that you had to write your name on the sign-up list before it was full. Many other people had visited the camp every year, so they knew the system, but I was a rookie. By the time I discovered that the list was making its rounds, I was too late to be included. My little heart sank to my toes as a sob rose in my throat. Hoping for mercy, I talked to the wranglers, but there were only ten horses available and all the spots were filled. Fighting tears, I added my name as an alternate and hoped for the best.

The ride was on Saturday, the last day of camp, so all week I prayed and hoped for a miracle, begging God to make a way for me to spend a whole day with the horses. Just before the event, an older teenage girl approached me. She was one of the "cool people." Her auburn hair was naturally curly . . . not permed like mine. I was slightly in awe that she would even speak to me.

"So, I heard that you wanted to go on the day-trip horseback ride," she said.

I nodded with a woebegone look as only a thirteen-year-old can do.

"Well, my family has horses so I can ride anytime. I signed up for the day trip, but I was thinking you could take my place."

Throwing my arms around this girl, I simply couldn't say thank you enough! She became my hero. The generosity of her gift was more than I could take in . . . she didn't have to give up her spot for me . . . but she did. Her only reason was to express the joy of giving.

That Saturday, I was in my element. We rode horses through the Colorado mountains, stopping for lunch in golden aspen forests. The head wrangler, a young woman, caught my attention when she shared her personal testimony over the picnic. My faith was stirred. The earlier act of generosity had planted another seed of faith in my heart. Today, no one has to tell me that the practice of giving pays off. Even little things matter . . . in bigger ways than we can imagine.

Christmas Morning

Another reason for giving is that God gives back to those who give. In fact, he gives *more* in return and promises that gifts to his kingdom will come back around! The whole spirit of generosity can be defeated if we're "giving to get." But false motives don't change God's heart: he still loves to give, and he rewards those who give willingly from a pure heart.

Participating in the Father's generosity is like celebrating Christmas with lots of gifts: you don't give gifts in order to get them, but you join in the spirit of giving when you choose to give. The true heart of a giver offers a gift with no strings attached and no obligation to give, because that would defeat the purpose of a heartfelt gift. However, in a loving family, we know we'll receive gifts in return, because that's part of the celebration, and no one is excluded.

The generosity of Christmas is a tiny glimpse into the heart of the Father *all the time*. Not only does he give to us, but he encourages us to live generous lives, knowing heaven's response toward a giving heart is to reward the giver. He says,

> Give, and it will be given to you: good measure, pressed down, shaken together, and running over will be put into your bosom. For with the same measure that you use, it will be measured back to you.
>
> Luke 6:38

The measure that we give to others enables that same gift to come back to us in remarkable ways. God loves to give, and when we tap into the spirit of giving, the kindness and generosity of others returns to us when we least expect it. God gives gifts all year long, and just like on Christmas morning, we always get more than we give.

Our Father loves when we give, and each gift is important to him. Just as a good parent adores gifts from each of their children, God loves when his kids give to him from their hearts! Sometimes we may feel like we have very little to offer, but Jesus told us that no gift is too small for him to notice. In fact, even a cup of cold water given in his name is noted in heaven. He said,

> And whoever gives one of these little ones only a cup of cold water in the name of a disciple, assuredly, I say to you, he shall by no means lose his reward.
>
> Matthew 10:42

The spiritual discipline of giving is something that everyone can do, no matter how much or how little we think we have. To our Father, every gift is valued and noted when given from a heart of love.

Three Gifts to Give

Most people are able to offer gifts of time, money, and talent. We are all given an equal portion of twenty-four hours in a day, most of us have a salary or income, and God has invested talents inside each one of us. Your local church is a great place to start giving! Being part of a thriving community where you have a vital part to play is so healthy for spiritual growth. However, the discipline of giving represents a lifestyle that can be used wherever we are, inside or out of the church. By unpacking each one of these, we'll discover that we each have an amazing amount to offer.

Gifts of Time

Recently I was challenged by the importance of the gift of time during an overseas mission trip. I had been to this particular nation several times to film and minister, and it had often been a fast-paced schedule. This time, I was booked to minister in a number of churches, but there were large gaps of empty space between the dates, so I had more time to simply hang out with the locals.

Several people made comments similar to this: "Rebecca, so many Americans come to our country and minister. We love them and what they bring, but they never connect with us in person. It's so good to *spend time* with you on this trip! Thank you."

What a deeply humbling and moving comment! We can get so wrapped up in our ambition to accomplish things that it's easy to forget how valuable the gift of time is. As you may have heard, one way of spelling "love" is T-I-M-E, and this cross-cultural, multigenerational gift simply requires a deposit of a few hours into someone's life. What a treasure to be able to build relationships over an hour at a coffee shop!

> The gift of shared time
> goes both ways . . .
>
> Our souls made rich
> by moments
> spent together.

On this same mission trip, I left one country to minister in another. As I boarded the plane after a teary hug from a friend, my head was spinning with the sorrow of saying goodbye. Upon my arrival, my new hosts offered to take me hiking in the mountains near their home. The simple gift of time toward a stranger was exactly the balm my travel-weary soul needed. We hiked to waterfalls, drank from clear streams, and took deep breaths of forest air. My mind shifted from a blurred haze into fresh focus. I can't tell you how much their gift of time meant to me!

It's easy to forget

how valuable

the gift of time is.

As you offer the gift of time, think about where you could invest it in order to make a difference in someone's life. Maybe it's as simple as volunteering at a local ministry, reaching out to a younger person in the faith and inviting them to spend time with you, or having coffee with a friend who's going through a rough time. Your gift of time can make a world of difference to them.

Gifts of Money

Jesus mentioned money in roughly 15 percent of his preaching, and eleven out of his thirty-nine parables involved money in some way. The ten talents, the widow's mite, the unjust steward, the coin with the portrait of Caesar—they all have to do with finances, reminding us that the way we handle money is a part of our spiritual journey. In the Old Testament, the Jewish people were called to give funds as an act of worship. The first thing God told Moses when he entered into the burning cloud on Mount Sinai was to take up an offering for the tabernacle, and there was such a massive response that they had to tell the people to stop giving! Later, tithes and offerings in the temple were the means that kept the doors open to their center of worship.

Today, money still offers a great opportunity to worship God; in fact, Jesus said that we can use the finances of this world to build up treasure in heaven. Someday our lives on earth will end, and we won't get to take a single penny into the afterlife, but if we use our finances well during our time on earth, we'll be building up treasure in the world to come.

> Sell what you have and give alms; provide yourselves money bags which do not grow old, a treasure in the heavens that does not fail, where no thief approaches nor moth destroys. For where your treasure is, there your heart will be also.
>
> Luke 12:33–34

This Scripture highlights a great point: when you are investing your life into God's kingdom and choosing to live generously, you have so much to look forward to. It's amazing to watch people's stress levels go up when the stock market crashes, especially if they've invested all their finances into the system of this world. However, if you're giving into God's kingdom, you can be sure that he'll meet your needs and your reward will be safely stored in heaven, where no earth-shattering crisis can touch it.

When considering how much money to give into God's kingdom, the choice is completely up to you. The 10 percent tithe to your church is a great place to start—I've watched God bless people because of their obedience to give that amount off their paycheck right away, and it's a good way to practice the spiritual discipline of giving with finances. Or you may want to explore more options like the famous builder and professor R. G. LeTourneau did. He created bulldozers and earth-moving equipment for the Allies of World War II and then went on to establish an international company. A strong believer, he decided to tithe 90 percent of his income and live off of 10 percent, giving the rest to missions.[4] LeTourneau University, the private Christian college that he founded, is one of the few faith-based colleges equipped with a flight program, and I have personal friends among the graduates who are missionary pilots in third world countries. What a powerful legacy of giving!

Some of my first lessons in giving took place when I was a young adult living in the backwoods of East Texas, where someone invested a financial gift that helped to jump-start a whole new phase of my life. My family lived on the backside of nowhere, with only a dial-up modem and very little connection to the outside world. However, my dream was to print a faith-based magazine and publish it every month. I had a massive laser printer that looked like a small army tank, so I put it to use for my little magazine. Sometimes I included music CDs with songs written and recorded in our home studio. I was surprised to see that people really seemed to enjoy the idea, and they sent little donations from time to time that helped cover the cost of ink and paper.

One day, I received a letter from an old friend I hadn't seen in years. When I tore open the envelope, ten $100 bills fell into my hand, given from a single mother on my mailing list. My mouth dropped open, and my eyes blurred with tears. "I'm sowing into your ministry," she wrote, "and this money is a seed!" I was stunned by the $1,000 gift, especially because I knew it came from someone who didn't have a lot of extra money. As my ministry expanded, I used her gift to purchase a full-length keyboard, using it at ministry events for over ten years. Many people were led in worship and beautiful things happened because of that woman's gift! Her gift was a seed that not only encouraged and boosted my faith but also helped spread God's kingdom.

Her letter brought up a great point: *We give to be a part of a harvest.* Not only do we reflect our Father and participate in his service when we give, but he promises a harvest from the seeds we sow. Since that day, there have been times when I've been led by the Lord to give because I know there's a harvest ahead and I want to be part of it. If we see potential for the expansion of God's kingdom in a person or ministry, we get to be a part of the lives they touch when we help make it happen with our finances.

Gifts of Talent

God loves to give good gifts, and he created us with certain natural talents and abilities. Using those talents for God is a great way to practice following him, but it can actually be a trickier topic than it may seem. For some people, using your talents for God can be as simple as finding someone in need or a ministry who can use your gifts. For others, especially highly gifted and talented people, the path can be a bit more difficult, because we know we're called to something specific, but it's often hard to know how to get there. Over the years, I've watched people point out famous musicians or sports players and wistfully say, "If only they would become followers of Christ, think of how much impact they would have for God's kingdom!"

In theory, I agree, because I believe our talents were given to us by God and we should use them for his glory. The difficulty is this: *God doesn't always select our obvious gifts for his service.* Many of his most talented followers go through seasons of wrestling with their desire to be used by God until they lay everything before him and simply allow him to choose how to use them. As someone who is very creative, at times I've struggled with wanting to use one particular set of talents and eventually realizing it just wasn't the skill set God wanted to use right then.

> God seeks
> availability
> above our
> earthly skills.
>
> He uses gifts
> he's placed in us
> as we avail
> ourselves to him.

Recently I was chatting with my mentors, bestselling authors Bill and Pam Farrel, who have penned over fifty books and offer relationship coaching to a wide variety of audiences. In my opinion, they're prime examples of how people with passion can invest their talents in God's kingdom and see a vast harvest of fruit, so I asked them to offer tips on how to discern God's will on this topic.

"When you're trying to figure out your creative gifts," Bill began, "you'll recognize that not everything you're good at is where God puts his favor. It's one of the ways God builds humility into the picture of our lives—he doesn't bless everything we're good at. Instead, he blesses areas that he's called us to."

Bill shared the example of the apostle Paul, who seemed to have all the talents required for a ministry to the Jews: an understanding of Hebrew Scriptures, a prior history with the leaders, and the ability to extend the gospel in a way they could understand. The only problem was that every time he spoke to them, they got mad, started riots, and wanted to arrest him. God's favor was clearly not on the obvious ministry Paul could have had based on his talents. Yet, every time he spoke to the gentiles, churches sprang up as a result of his teaching. Eventually, it seems that Paul came to grips with his calling, and toward the end of his life he started calling himself an "apostle to the gentiles." In his heart, he longed to minister to his countrymen, the Jews, yet God had a different plan. Paul had to discover that the calling of God was not the obvious one, although his many talents were used in very different ways to bring God glory.

"For me, this process has been both glorious and agonizing," Bill said with open honesty. "I remember when I was pastoring and investing a ridiculous amount of hours trying to grow the church, and the church was only moving by inches. Then I would go do a relationship training conference with Pam, put very little effort into the weekend, and stuff happened. People were tearing up divorce papers, giving their hearts to Christ, and all this vibrant work was taking place! I would come home and say, *Really, God? I go do a conference and you do all this amazing stuff, and I pour all this effort into the church and it barely moves!* I had to wrestle: was I going to accept where God's favor was moving, or was I going to force where I wanted his hand to move?"

"Pastoring the church was like pushing a snowball *uphill*," Pam chimed in, "and our Love-Wise ministry was like riding a snowball *downhill!*"

"It was very humbling," Bill said, "when I told God, 'If I have to choose between pastoring and doing conferences with Pam, I'll choose the conferences, because I see your hand of favor.'"

Part of the key to giving our talents to God is that we simply step out and start somewhere. We can't just bury our gifts; we put them to work. If you're a singer, try out for the worship team. If you're an accountant, consider helping someone in need with their taxes. Poets, start putting your work on social media and letting your light shine to the world! As you prayerfully move forward, ask God to show you where the place of his blessing is, and then watch for opportunities to prayerfully invest your energy into those areas. When you start seeing him touch hearts, you'll recognize the specialized way he's called you to give! Your unique calling is different than anyone else's, and investing it into God's kingdom is a powerful gift you can offer.

Giving with Passion

Someone once told me, "To find out where you should give, discover which ministries you are passionate about, and sow into them."

As I pondered this thought, I started making a mental list of what moved my heart. *I'm really heartbroken by sex trafficking and the abuse of women*, I realized. By giving into ministries that were bringing freedom to trafficked women, I realized that my funds were being used to help an issue I was passionate about. It made me even more excited to give! Later, I discovered a particular nation that I felt connected to and decided to support a ministry that reaches out to the poor within that region. My heart was involved, I knew my gift mattered, and I could read the updates on how my gifts were touching lives in the place I was passionate about. Not only that, but I knew that the Lord was pleased with my giving.

> If you help the poor, you are lending to the LORD—
> and he will repay you!
>
> Proverbs 19:17 NLT

If our acts of giving are building up credit with the God of the universe, that's a pretty good investment! When we give with pure motives, he makes sure that our generosity always comes back around.

Your Turn

- List some of the things you can offer when giving. Include gifts of friendship, finances, time, talent, cooking, etc.
- What are some ways you can invest these things into God's kingdom and your spiritual community?
- Are there any ministries you especially feel passionate about giving to?
- Take a moment to pray over where God would have you give, and ask for his leading.

Spiritual Practice

Make a list of things you feel like you can give. Include areas of time, money, and talent. Then write down some ways you can give. Maybe it's poking a hole in a jar for extra change, putting it on your kitchen counter, and having a place to donate the coins when the jar is full. Or maybe it's volunteering at your church. Or creating a work of art and giving it away. Or going on a mission trip to serve the church in another country. What are some ways the generosity of God can be displayed in your life?

ELEVEN

Fasting

FIX YOUR ATTENTION ON CHRIST

One time I dated a man who took me to a scenic overlook with a dazzling view of the ocean. He then proceeded to scroll through his phone, leaving me wondering why he brought me there in the first place. I'll be honest: it was annoying. We were pretty good friends, so I casually mentioned that he seemed rather preoccupied with his own world at the moment. To his credit, he immediately said, "Sorry about that." Putting down his phone, he shifted his attention squarely on me, making eye contact. "Okay, I'm fully present!"

We ended up having a good time because he made the effort to check out of his world and intentionally focus on the person in front of him.

If you've ever been on a date with someone who's constantly on their phone, you'll know that it doesn't create great momentum for communication. Maybe they have a good reason to be absorbed in their work, but it takes the focus off the relationship, right?

While we live on earth, there will always be "good reasons" that can distract us from our relationship with God. The war for our attention wages on social media, in opportunities at work, in creative projects, and even within our families. When this world screams for our presence, one of the best ways to intentionally focus on God is to practice fasting. When we fast as a spiritual practice, we're like the person who puts their phone away, locks eyes with the Friend across the table, and says, "In this moment, I choose you. No distractions—I'm here to listen, talk, or whatever you need. Right now, it's all about you."

Essentially, it's doing what a good friend does when they choose to invest in a relationship: we set down the things of this world to focus on the One we love. Jesus is waiting for connection, and he loves when we fix our eyes on his face. Fasting is a great way to do this.

Fasting also prepares us for the divine adventure Christ has planned for us. Fueling our faith, it helps us connect with heaven's supply for our needs rather than our earthly resources.

> In a culture that fights
> to satisfy the flesh,
> fasting says to God . . .
>
> *We hunger*
> *for something*
> *food can't fill,*
> *money can't buy,*
> *and the world*
> *can never satisfy.*

By abstaining from a few earthly needs or joys, fasting proves that we're serious about deliberately shifting our vision from earth toward things God cares about and that we want to be strengthened and sustained by him rather than just our daily meals. Fasting creates an opportunity for God to meet with us, to become our

When we fast as a spiritual practice, we're like the person who puts their phone away, locks eyes with the Friend across the table, and says, "In this moment, I choose you."

daily bread, emotional strength, and the peace the core of our being longs for. Instead of filling up on things of the world, we abstain from what we normally turn to for food or enjoyment and ask him to fill us instead.

Fasting—Breaking It Down

Fasting is a biblical practice that pre-dates Christianity and was often practiced by the Jewish people as a way of devotion and worship to God. It helped them live set-apart lives not because they desired to be legalistic or overly spiritual but because fasting was a way to plug into the power behind their faith—the belief that God's truth was more real than their everyday lives—and they wanted to connect with his reality. These were the "Jedi warriors" of Scripture, men and women who chose to deny themselves a few pleasures in order to tune their ears toward God's heart and calling. Scriptural characters like Elijah, Anna, Moses, and Esther all used fasting to overcome issues that we still fight today: depression, loneliness, need for direction, and spiritual opposition.

Today, as the media screams in our ears, and the appetites of our humanity promise to satisfy the longings of our heart, fasting enables us to focus on the eternal truths of God, who has chosen us for a close connection with himself. If we are longing for a deeper connection with Christ or are asking God to meet some needs in our lives, fasting is a powerful tool we can use.

In my personal life, I've discovered that fasting is like putting my prayer life into "light speed." If I want an answer, need wisdom for a creative project, or am preparing to go on a mission trip, fasting and prayer is a powerful way to tap into the resources of heaven. It's a way to show God that I care about his work and perspective even more than my next meal, and it prepares the way for him to show himself strong in whatever I'm asking him for. To be honest, fasting is addictive! It's like being in a constant place of intercession, where God's ears are especially tuned to my prayers because I'm making the intentional effort to pursue him in this biblical way. There's so much joy that comes from this spiritual practice!

In this chapter, we'll unpack what the Scriptures tell us about fasting and outline some practical ways we can implement it today. Let's start by learning what Jesus taught his followers, and we'll discover how we can apply his words as modern-day disciples.

Jesus and Fasting

Fasting is one of those spiritual disciplines that Jesus specifically gave to his disciples after he went to heaven. While he was on earth, there was no distance between him and his followers; they could talk to him about whatever they wanted, anytime and anywhere. However, we don't have the luxury of the physical presence of Jesus, so we have to lean in close to the relationship for an intimate connection, and fasting is one way we do that.

There's a fascinating account in the Gospels that gives a window of insight into how we are called to fast. When Jesus was on earth with his disciples, he taught about fasting, but they didn't practice it. This bothered some people of the day because fasting was practiced very regularly by Jewish rabbis and their followers, and it was part of their duties of worship as a nation. For instance, each year the entire nation of Israel completely abstained from food and drink during the Day of Atonement, fasting as an act of repentance and humility and asking God to forgive their sins. The leaders had extra days of fasting, during which time the rabbis (or "teachers") refused to wash their faces, wanting to look as disheveled as possible so everyone else knew they were paying tribute to God. To the first-century Jews, fasting was a normal practice for spiritual leaders and groups, highly practiced and highly praised.

So when Jesus talked about fasting but didn't practice it with his disciples, this raised some eyebrows for those watching him. Later we'll see that Jesus practiced fasting privately, but at this point in his ministry, he didn't require his disciples to fast, and he certainly didn't go around looking disheveled when he fasted.

> Then they said to Him, "Why do the disciples of John fast often and make prayers, and likewise those of the Pharisees, but Yours eat and drink?"
>
> And He said to them, "Can you make the friends of the bridegroom fast while the bridegroom is with them? But the days will come when the bridegroom will be taken away from them; then they will fast in those days."
>
> Luke 5:33–35

When Jesus was on earth, his disciples didn't need to fast because they were having face-to-face encounters with God every day. Their requests were immediately responded to—they had no need to pray for the forgiveness of sin, because the Redeemer was standing in front of them. However, he said that his disciples *would* fast when he was not with them, foretelling that spiritual fasting would be a part of his followers' practices of worship after he ascended to heaven. During the times when Jesus was not physically with them, fasting would become a way his disciples could tune out earth and focus on the heartbeat of heaven.

Fasting for Whom?

Jesus also shifted cultural ideas about fasting, having some strong, poignant words for rabbis who used it to make a public display of their devotion. Instead, he taught that this spiritual discipline was a private practice between the individual and God. While the Pharisees made a show of their misery while fasting, Christ taught us that the goal of fasting was to interact with the Father, and his response was the one that mattered.

> And when you fast, don't make it obvious, as the hypocrites do, for they try to look miserable and disheveled so people will admire them for their fasting. I tell you the truth, that is the only reward they will ever get. But when you fast, comb your hair and wash your face. Then no one will notice that you are fasting, except your Father, who knows what you do in private. And your Father, who sees everything, will reward you.
>
> Matthew 6:16–18 NLT

Jesus was clear that fasting was not meant to blow our own horn and say, "Hey, everyone! I'm fasting. Look how spiritual I am!"

The purpose of fasting is *relationship* with God, not calling attention to what you are doing, as if God could be "arm candy" for you to hang out with. Getting to know God is a reward in itself—you don't have to brag about it, and your life will prove the results.

Jesus also taught that fasting and prayer is a way for spiritual breakthrough and power over the enemy of our souls. When praying for the man overcome with demons, the disciples were not able to set him free, and they became frustrated. Jesus dealt with the situation quickly, delivering the man, and his bewildered disciples later asked, "Why couldn't we cast it out?"

Jesus gives them a lesson on faith, and then he makes the curious statement,

> However, this kind does not go out except by prayer and fasting.
>
> Matthew 17:21

Not only does fasting help build intimacy with the Father, but it's also a strategy for spiritual warfare. It's the secret weapon of spiritual warriors who realize that they aren't strong enough to win the war but know they can call on the armies of heaven to do battle for them. When we fast to overcome spiritual strongholds in our lives or in the lives of others, incredible breakthrough can happen.

Fasting in the Church

After Jesus returned to heaven, the apostles implemented fasting as part of their lives of prayer. While they didn't fast for the forgiveness of sins like the Jews did, because Christ had fully satisfied that requirement on the cross, the early church practiced fasting when making big decisions, such as choosing and ordaining new leaders for the church.

> So when they had appointed elders in every church, and prayed with fasting, they commended them to the Lord in whom they had believed.
>
> Acts 14:23

Sometimes fasting was done as "ministry to the Lord," by simply thrusting other things aside to fix their gaze on Christ. From this place of focused prayer and worship, the Holy Spirit gave clear directions about what they should do. In one case, the Lord called Paul and Barnabas as missionaries to the nations while believers from Antioch were ministering to Christ in this way. They didn't stop fasting when they heard God speak: instead, they fasted even more and prayed for these two men who were about to take a wild adventure to share Christ with the world.

> As they ministered to the Lord and fasted, the Holy Spirit said, "Now separate to Me Barnabas and Saul for the work to which I have called them." Then, having fasted and prayed, and laid hands on them, they sent them away.
>
> Acts 13:2–3

As a result, Paul and Barnabas traveled to many places, starting churches and seeing God move in powerful ways. Since fasting and prayer brings breakthrough and spiritual freedom, I've sometimes wondered if part of their success was due to the fasting ministry of the group of disciples who had such incredible lives of prayer. Regardless, their intercession jump-started a massive mission trip that God used to bring the gospel to the nations in a powerful way.

After starting many churches, the apostle Paul later mentioned fasting in one of his follow-up letters to the young groups of believers. In his advice to married couples, he advocated that fasting was often practiced by members of the early church, not just their leaders. He suggested that they should remain consistent in their intimate relations, except when they both agreed upon times of fasting and prayer. This was another way they could lay aside even the good things in life to completely focus on God for a brief time of fasting.

> Do not deprive one another except with consent for a time, that you may give yourselves to fasting and prayer; and come together again so that Satan does not tempt you because of your lack of self-control.
>
> 1 Corinthians 7:5

Whether you were a new believer or spiritual leader, fasting was recognized as a vital practice for the church. It didn't die out after the first century, since we have records that many of the next generation of leaders and desert fathers practiced fasting as a means to further their spiritual growth. It was their way of setting aside the things of this world to fix their attention on Christ, and they encouraged their followers to do the same.

Face Time with God

During times of fasting and prayer, we gain clarity for our calling, identity, and spiritual authority. Scripture gives us a few accounts of how individuals grew in their spiritual life by leaps and bounds when they practiced this spiritual discipline. Through their lives, we glimpse some of the powerful reasons and benefits of connecting with God in this way. I've condensed their stories here, but you can read the full accounts by looking up the Scripture references.

Moses, Face-to-Face with God (Deut. 9:9–18)

The Ten Commandments were given to Moses during a forty-day fast, when God specifically called him to hike up the desert mountain of Sinai and spend some alone time there. Over forty days, God met him face-to-face and released a powerful strategy on how to build a system of worship for the entire nation of Israel. It reminds us that we can fast for direction and strategy when in a "wilderness" season, asking God for vision and his plans for our life.

Anna, Gaining Discernment (Luke 2:36–38)

When the eight-day-old baby Jesus was brought to the bustling temple for his dedication, only two people discerned that he was the Messiah who would save the world. One of them was the prophetess Anna, an elderly widow who lived in the temple and constantly served God in fasting and prayer. Scripture tells us that she rejoiced to see him and spread the word of his arrival to others who were looking for redemption in Jerusalem. When we practice a life of fasting and prayer, God can give us discernment into things that are easily overlooked because we are cultivating a life of listening to his voice.

Jesus, Overcoming Temptation (Luke 4:1–13)

Before his public ministry began, Jesus was baptized in the Jordan River and immediately went into the wilderness for forty days of fasting and prayer. We're not told what happened during that fast, but afterward we're told that he was very hungry. The devil appeared to him and mockingly began to tempt him to rely on his power to meet his own hunger. Each time, Jesus adopted God's perspective instead of the temptations of the world. Forty days of fasting had focused his soul, enabling him to fix his eyes on heaven's calling and not be deceived by the devil's lies.

In the same way, God gives us power to overcome temptation when we use fasting as a means to fix our eyes on him, choosing to connect with his perspective of us and his call on our lives and defeating the enemy.

Daniel, Praying for a Nation (Dan. 10:2–14)

As a refugee in the strange land of Babylon, Daniel fasted for three weeks, praying for a way to return the nation of Israel to their homeland. During this time, he fasted from meat, wine, and customary anointing with oil as he laid his petition before God.

On day twenty-four, a fiery angel visited him with a message. The angel was so powerful that Daniel was knocked unconscious! Laying his hand on the prophet, the angel said, "O Daniel, a man greatly beloved, understand the words that I speak to you, and stand upright, for I have now been sent to you."

The angel told Daniel that the response to his prayer had been delayed because of a heavenly battle but that the message had finally arrived. Although it took a little while for the answer to appear, Daniel's prayers were rewarded by a personal message of God's love and an answer of how God was going to bring the nation of Israel back to their own land. We too can fast and pray for our nation, and even if there is a bigger battle going on than we can imagine, we know that God hears our prayers.

Elijah, Overcoming Depression (1 Kings 19:1–18)

When confronted by murderous Queen Jezebel, Elijah fled into the wilderness. He had just emerged from an amazing mountain-top experience where fire fell from heaven and the nation of Israel had been stirred from their complacency to destroy their idols and worship God again. However, when Jezebel sent a messenger promising swift revenge, his courage gave way to despair. Sadly, not a single person rose to defend him, and Elijah spent forty days fasting and seeking the face of God.

"I'm the only prophet left," he complained to God, "and they seek my life too!"

Bracing himself for God's reply, Elijah hid in a cave on Mount Sinai. A mighty wind swept the wilderness, breaking the rocks in pieces . . . then an earthquake shook the land, and a fire swept the mountain. However, God's response was not in any of these great displays of power. Finally, a still, small voice spoke to the prophet, giving him the perspective he needed.

When we're faced with a spiritual battle, sometimes it's easy to feel overwhelmed, isolated, and that we're the only person still faithful to God. Stepping away for times of fasting and prayer allows God to shift our focus and give us hope for the future.

Esther, Protection and Safety (Esther 4:14–16)

Chosen as queen for her beauty and grace, Esther rose to royalty in the Babylonian palace. However, the truth about her Jewish identity was kept secret because the Israelites were refugees in the foreign nation. When the political leader Haman tried to bring genocide upon the Jews, Esther's uncle pleaded with her to intercede on their behalf to the king.

"Who knows," he told her, "perhaps you were come into the kingdom for such a time as this!"

"Go, gather the Jews in the city," Esther replied, knowing that it could mean death for her to approach the throne unbidden by the king. "Fast and pray for three days, and my maidens and I will do the same. Then I will go to the king. If I perish, I perish."

God's response to prayer, fasting, and courage was to turn the situation around, protecting the Jews and exposing Haman's wicked schemes, so that the entire Jewish population in Babylon was saved. Like Esther, we too can fast for protection and safety during difficult times.

Paul, Sincere Repentance (Acts 9:1–19)

The apostle Paul used fasting as a means to show heartfelt repentance to God. When Paul (then called Saul) was traveling on a road toward Damascus, planning to persecute and kill Christians, a bright light shone from heaven and the voice of Jesus called to him. Blinded by the light and stricken by the fact that his zeal had led him so wrongly, Paul spent the next three days fasting. Another disciple named Ananias was sent by God to pray for Paul. God healed Paul's eyes, and the new believer was baptized to announce his new faith in Jesus.

Like Paul, we can fast and pray when convicted of sin, asking the Lord to cleanse our conscience. We don't have to fast in order to be forgiven, because Jesus already gave that to us, but sometimes fasting is useful to "reset" when we've sinned against the Lord. Purity, the right motives, and a mind that has a clean conscience can all be pursued through fasting and prayer.

John the Baptist, a Nazirite (Acts 18:18)

The Nazirite vow was an Old Testament fast that required abstaining from wine and grape juice and sometimes involved letting your hair grow long. Before John the Baptist was conceived, Gabriel the angel told John's father that the boy would be a Nazirite and that he was set apart for God in this special way. Part of the massive call on John's life was to fast and pray in order to prepare the way for the coming of Jesus.

Sometimes this vow was made for just a season rather than a lifetime. The apostle Paul also mentions shaving his head because of a vow, which shows us that the Nazirite fast was being practiced even in New Testament times. Like he did these men, God may ask us to abstain for a season from something that is acceptable to society, like wine, to represent a call to holiness and preparation in our lives.

Fasting Tips

Here are some tips for practicing fasting in your own life. First, recognize that there are several types of fasting methods offered in Scripture, and there's no single, precise way to go about it. While the most common way of fasting is to give up food and sometimes water, many people have health restrictions that don't make this the best option. If you want to do an extreme fast like this, always assess your medical health to make sure you're able to practice it in a safe way. Most medical doctors applaud fasting if there are no health constraints, and occasional fasting is actually a very good means to balance your body. However, be sure to check with your doctor if you have any questions. If you'd rather fast from something besides food and water, there are ways of giving up something else that is meaningful to you and fast that way instead. Here are a few ideas:

A Daniel Fast

The prophet Daniel gave up wine and meat for his fast, and God sent an angel in response.[1] If you don't want to abstain from entire meals, choose a few things from the menu that would be meaningful to you and fast from those instead. God seems to honor even a partial food fast if our heart is in the right place.

Juice Fast

Completely abstaining from food can be hard, so a good "starter fast" may be as simple as drinking fruit and vegetable juices throughout the day instead of eating food. And of course, water is included as well. My family fasted often when I was a child, so

I decided to try a juice fast for a day when I was about nine years old. This type of fast is safe and healthy for most people.

Complete Fast

When abstaining from all food and water, this fast should only be practiced by healthy people for a maximum of three days, otherwise serious health issues can occur. I've done this fast on several occasions, and it's always a challenge, but most people stop feeling hungry after about twenty-four hours because their stomach starts to shrink. You may experience low energy, so it's a good idea to plan this type of fast if you have several days to completely devote yourself to prayer and minimal exertion.

Like Jesus and Moses, people still practice forty-day fasts on water or limited food, but there's a lot of education and careful planning that must happen first. Don't dive into this kind of fast unless you are specifically called by the Lord, and make sure you're doing it in a healthy way!

Alternative Fasts

While biblical fasts predominately include giving up food and water, there are other ways you can fast. Refraining from social media, movies, or other activities that you would normally do as entertainment or relaxation can work as well. Make sure you spend more time in prayer instead of doing that activity.

Corporate Fasting

Sometimes a church will fast as a group before making a big decision or in preparation for a new season. As we saw in the book of Acts, God moved powerfully when the church fasted! Having a prayer partner can be helpful as you start your fasting journey: ask a friend if they will fast with you or at least cover you in prayer as you do.

Write It Down

As you explore fasting, it's a good idea to keep a journal. During your fast, write down anything that God brings to mind, such as

- anyone you need to forgive, or ask forgiveness of
- people to pray for
- specific needs for direction or clarity in your life
- prayer for protection
- needs and provision
- requests for deliverance and spiritual breakthrough
- national prayers
- a desire for deeper intimacy with Jesus

As you fast, spend time in God's Word. It's amazing how the Scriptures often come alive when fasting! Playing worship music, creating artwork, or doing Bible studies can be great options during this time too. Write down any questions you have, and note any answers or things God lays on your heart during this time. Sometimes the response to a fast may come a short time afterward, so it's good to watch for breakthroughs in the days after your fast and make note of them. When you complete your fast, you'll be able to flip through the notes you've written, be reminded of your journey, and see what God has done!

Your Turn

- Are there any benefits from fasting that you'd like to see in your spiritual life?
- In what ways could fasting enable you to focus on God?
- What could fasting look like for you? A juice fast? A media fast? Or food?
- What length of fast would you take?

Spiritual Practice

Plan your fast! Think through your calendar and see when would be a good time to set apart several days for fasting and prayer. Depending on the type of fast, you don't have to stop work during this time, unless it's an extreme one. If you feel the need, ask several close spiritual friends to pray with you as you fast. Make a clear outline of your goals and prayer requests, and block out some extra time to spend in prayer with God. Journal your journey, and see what he will do!

TWELVE

Worship

CONNECT WITH THE MASTER

It was Good Friday, and bells were ringing all over the city. Balancing a backpack full of cameras on my shoulder, I climbed the winding staircase in Jerusalem to visit the historical site of the Upper Room, traditionally thought to be the location of the Last Supper and the place where the Holy Spirit came on Pentecost. I had no idea that a divine adventure was waiting for me on the other side of the door . . .

Upon entering the room, the noise of the city quickly hushed with the thud of the door behind me. A new sound met my ears. Fervent singing in a foreign language echoed through the stone chamber, filling the pillared room with a cappella music. A tour group of Asian believers had decided to hold their worship service in the stone room, and I happened upon their group. I stealthily wound my way to the back of the room, setting my backpack on the stone floor and lowering to my knees.

It wasn't the melody or the sound of their songs that caught my attention. It was their indescribable passion that had touched a chord of worship I'd seldom heard before. The air was electric, as if the hosts of heaven decided to join the vocals. Suddenly they broke into the words "Alleluia, alleluia," and I was able to join in the familiar chorus, adding my sound to the international choir of praise.

Tears pricked my eyes, but I was almost afraid to shed them, not wanting to interrupt this sacred moment. Soon the service ended, they resumed their Asian dialect among themselves, and I had no idea what was being said. They walked out of the building, and I was left alone to ponder the experience. I'll never forget that moment with believers from another nation, where the only shared word was *Alleluia*, but the atmosphere was so charged with the presence of God that you couldn't help but worship. I felt it in the air . . . the passion . . . the vibrant sense of souls touching heaven . . . and heaven's response. Worship was a tangible thing, like the worn stones of that ancient place.

Master and Dog

To discover the spiritual practice of worship, we have to start with the question, *What is worship?* Is it a music genre? Or a few songs on Sunday morning? According to the Scripture, those who discover the authentic definition of worship carry a quality of such great value that God himself actually seeks them out. Jesus said,

> But the hour is coming, and now is, when the true worshipers will worship the Father in spirit and truth; for the Father is seeking such to worship Him.

> John 4:23

If we unpack the definition of *worship* in Scripture, we'll discover some beautiful keys in the kinds of worship that profoundly unlock our divine adventure.

My friend Barbara in Scotland tells a story that beautifully illustrates one scriptural definition of worship. Her golden-brown cocker spaniel named Fiona lived in kennels and belonged to three owners before she was a year old. When Barbara adopted her, she drove the puppy to her home on the island of Arran, Scotland: a farmhouse on a hill overlooking miles of windswept Highland fields and the sparkling sea. On a walk with her new master, the pup was able to run completely free for the first time in her life. Her ears flapping in the crisp Scottish breeze, Fiona leapt in the grass around Barbara, yelping and even falling over with excitement and delight.

Soon, Fiona became completely devoted to her new owner. When Barbara had to leave home, the dog greeted her return with wild abandon, wagging her tail and running circles around her beloved owner until she collapsed with exhaustion. If she could speak, Fiona might say, *I am so happy you are home again! It's you I adore, and I need you to keep me secure and safe—I love you and I know you love me! You rescued me and set me free to be who I was meant to be.*

Now, after thirteen years at the farm, Fiona's sight and hearing are not as strong as they were in the early days, so Barbara communicates in other ways with her beloved dog. She recently told me, "To say hello, I cradle her silky golden face in my hands, look straight into her eyes, and softly blow on her face. It's my way of saying without words, *You are okay, and you don't have to be afraid.* She loves it so much—she could stay in that place forever!"

This story offers a beautiful description of the most often used word for "worship" in the New Testament. *Strong's Concordance* defines the Greek word *proskuneo* this way: "to kiss, like a dog licking his master's hand." This word is the most commonly used term for worship in the Greek manuscripts, and it's used fifty-four times in the New Testament. If you can imagine the wagging tail and adoring doggy eyes of a pet who runs to press his nose into his master's hand, you've just visualized the word for worship! That passion to be close to the Master, exuberance to find and follow him, and longing for close connection is exactly what a friendly dog and a Jesus-worshiper have in common. Like Fiona's master, Barbara, Jesus has set us free and enables us to become all we are called to be, and our devotion and love for our Master can be beyond words.

Just as Barbara tenderly took her pup's face in hand, telling her that everything was going to be okay, Jesus responds to our worship in the most gracious of ways, calming our fears and giving us peace.

> Worship is . . .
> a two-way
> conversation.
>
> An intimate
> connection with the Lord
>
> Wherein his Presence
> comforts,
> strengthens,
> reassures us.

Scripture gives us another picture with a slightly different metaphor: the shepherd and sheep. Jesus, the Good Shepherd, knows and looks after each of his sheep, even those prone to wanderlust or moments of anxiety. He said,

> I am the good shepherd; and I know My sheep, and am known by My own.
>
> John 10:14

This heart-connection of knowing and being known is what true worship is all about, as we give God our adoration and receive his love! It starts with a grateful heart, acknowledging his love and redemption, and allowing ourselves to think about the amazing things he has done. Just like the little dog Fiona, we find ourselves resting in the care of the Master and receiving his peace.

Worship and Service

Another word translated "worship" in our English Bibles is the Greek word *latreuo*, meaning "a hired servant for menial labor, to minister (to God), serve, render religious homage, worship." The idea of Christian service, whether in full-time ministry or in mundane small tasks that honor God and serve his people, is also considered worship. This word is scattered throughout Scripture; used in the context of service within the temple or those redeemed saints who serve before the throne in heaven, it's mentioned twenty-one times throughout the New Testament and is translated both "serve" and "worship" in our English Bibles.

Our acts of service, when done from a heart of love for Christ, are considered worship to him. If you're the janitor in a church or fixing meals for the homeless at a downtown mission, your service counts! You don't have to have a great voice or play an instrument to be a worshiper—your motive is what matters to God, and he is looking for those who serve him from a pure heart of love.

The apostle Paul used this word to describe his lifestyle of worship and service to God when defending his faith to the Jews:

> But this I confess to you, that according to the Way which they call a sect, so I *worship* the God of my fathers, believing all things which are written in the Law and in the Prophets.
>
> Acts 24:14 (emphasis added)

This same Greek word for *worship* is mentioned a few chapters later when Paul was trapped in a ship on a stormy sea, and the sailors feared death and shipwreck. This word for *worship* is translated "serve" in this passage:

> For there stood by me this night an angel of the God to whom I belong and whom I *serve*, saying, "Do not be afraid, Paul; you must be brought before Caesar; and indeed God has granted you all those who sail with you."
>
> Acts 27:23–24 (emphasis added)

195

This heart-connection

of knowing and being

known is what true

worship is all about,

as we give God

our adoration and

receive his love!

In both Scriptures, a life of service to God was Paul's line of defense when criticized or in trouble: the God he served and worshiped with his life would defend him. This active worship was incredible ammunition when he was in danger, because his service was an obvious mark of faith and character, and God responded by coming to his rescue. In the same way, God loves to respond when we worship by serving him with our lives, and we can rest assured that our service never goes unnoticed by him.

Bowing Down

As we continue to unpack the true heart of worship, we discover a few other definitions that are just as true today as they were thousands of years ago when prophets of old penned the words. In the Old Testament, a Hebrew word for *worship* is *shachah*, meaning "to prostrate or bow oneself down in homage to royalty." In modern terms that means "to fall on your face before the king"! In a time of history when bowing to leaders was common and prostrating yourself before a king was a sign of honor, it makes sense that worship to God would be described as falling down before the King of Heaven in surrender to his sovereign right to rule.

There's another reason for the use of this word: people who deeply encounter God tend to fall on their faces! His glory, holiness, and power make humans feel incredibly puny in comparison. Moses, Joshua, Peter, John, and many others in Scripture fell on their faces when encountering the glory of God. Taking a knee in prayer or worship is a beautiful, biblical practice of honoring God, as mentioned in the Psalms:

> Oh come, let us worship and bow down;
> Let us kneel before the LORD our Maker.
> For He is our God,
> And we are the people of His pasture,
> And the sheep of His hand.
>
> Psalm 95:6–7

The book of Revelation records that angels and saints often bow before the majestic throne of God. Some church denominations have created moments of kneeling in their worship services, and this practice not only reminds us that the God we serve is a great King, but it also places us in the same position that worshipers take in heaven. By bowing, we express on earth the kind of thing that happens all the time in heaven as angels and elders bow down and cast their crowns at his feet.[1] The idea of bowing before God is a precious way of worshiping where we acknowledge that he is the King of kings and the one true God!

Ways to Praise

As we unpack these words for *worship*, notice what these definitions leave out: there's no mention of music or instruments! While music can be a means to express our heart of adoration or service, it's really the motive behind those actions that God is interested in.

> True worship
> does not require
> a stage
> a podium
> a microphone.
>
> It starts behind the scenes,
> within a heart
> of radical devotion
> to Jesus.
>
> True worship is
> serving others
> bowing down
> chasing the Master
> like a devoted puppy.

So if worship is an attitude of the heart and a way to serve, where does music come in? Like the epic soundtrack of a great movie, music is a powerful way to worship God because it's a great means to communicate passion. Rhythms, lyrics, and sounds draw out our emotions, enabling us to connect with the message of the person singing. This is why we call good singers "musical artists," because they use this art form to communicate in a moving way. When we worship with a song, we're using this emotional expression to release the cry of our heart to God.

Of course, you can go through the motions of singing a song about God and that doesn't mean you're worshiping. But if your heart is using music to release adoration to him through song, it's an incredible way to worship God and invite others to do the same. The unity and beauty of people singing together is one of the hallmarks of Christianity—believers all through the ages have written and sung songs together.

If we dig a little deeper into Scripture, we'll discover that the Hebrew words for *praise* are often connected with music. In fact, there are several words used within the book of Psalms that are all translated "praise" in our English language but have *different types of expressions* of praise within the Hebrew words. The Jewish people were highly experiential and demonstrative in their praise, and understanding their language helps us unpack some ways we can praise God too! Here are a few samples:

Hallel—Our word *hallelujah* comes from this word. It means "to be clear, to praise, to shine, to boast, to show, to rave, to celebrate, to be clamorously foolish." Basically, it means to throw a party for God, even to the point of looking silly. To boast of what he's done in our lives, put on a show about it, celebrate, and even rave about how good he is!

> *Praise* the LORD!
> *Praise*, O servants of the LORD,
> *Praise* the name of the LORD!
> Psalm 113:1 (emphasis added)

True worship is

serving others

bowing down

chasing the Master

like a devoted puppy.

Yadah—A verb with a root that means "the extended hand, to throw out the hand, therefore to worship with extended hand, to lift the hands." It's the idea of lifting up your hands while praising God, using motion as you express your praise.

> I will *praise* You, O Lord, among the peoples;
> I will sing to You among the nations.
>
> Psalm 57:9 (emphasis added)

Shabach—"To address in a loud tone," meaning to praise God with a shout. There are times when we sing or declare loudly the praises of God as we triumphantly declare his goodness. The following verse has two very different words for praise in it, although they are both translated "praise" in our English tongue.

> *Praise* the LORD, O Jerusalem!
> *Praise* your God, O Zion!
>
> Psalm 147:12 (emphasis added)

The first is *hallel*, and the second is *shabach*, so the verse could read something like this: "Boast, brag, and be clamorously foolish before the LORD, O Jerusalem! Shout loudly in praise to him, O Zion!"

Zamar—"To pluck the strings of an instrument; to sing, to praise with the voice; to celebrate in song and music." This word weaves the idea of music into the expression of praise, inviting people to praise God with a song.

> Be exalted, O LORD, in Your own strength!
> We will sing and *praise* Your power.
>
> Psalm 21:13 (emphasis added)

Tehillah—"To sing a hymn of praise." Our humble praises carry a magnetic effect of catching his attention and

turning his gaze. How he loves when we sing to him! God
enjoys songs of praise so much that he uses this word to
describe how his presence rests on our praises like a king
upon a throne!

> But You are holy,
> Enthroned in the *praises* of Israel.
>
> Psalm 22:3 (emphasis added)

Whether in a song, an honest prayer, or a life invested in service,
the expressions of our heart toward God matter and please him
so much. In fact, our times of worship are far more interactive
than we think, because worship and praise accomplish far more
than we realize. Scripture offers many stories of battles that were
won, people who were healed, and lives that were touched through
praise and worship.

> When we worship,
> God shows up,
> and his presence
> changes things!

Worship Well

To date, I've led worship on platforms around the world, sometimes to an audience of a thousand or more, and it's been wonderful to see people open their hearts to God and sense his presence during the worship. As much as I love those times, the most
meaningful moments have happened in out-of-the-way places that
I simply happened to stumble upon. One of those places was in
Northern Ireland, where fiery Irish saints had left a mark on the
soil that still can be seen today.

Earlier I mentioned the tour of Celtic Christian sites that I
helped lead all over Ireland, north and south. Another stop on the
program was Bangor Abbey, a thriving training center for mission-

aries during the Dark Ages. While I had always loved this historical site and had previously visited several times, I'd never been able to fully step past the mystique and discover why it was so beautiful. But on that trip, I had a remarkable experience that reminded me just how far the effect of our worship carries.

Bangor, a city just outside of Belfast, is a port that overlooks the Irish Sea. In the sixth century, a community of two to three thousand saints lived there together, taking turns leading worship and prayer twenty-four hours a day. This constant rhythm lasted between 150 and 300 years at Bangor, and the Latin antiphonary (or song-and-prayer book) has been preserved to this day. Passages of Scripture, original prayers and songs, and blessings were all included. This center was a university, training many students in the arts, geography, and arithmetic, as well as in reading the Scriptures. Bangor was called "The Light of the World," because many missionaries were sent across Europe from the shores of this Irish community, even crossing the Alps by foot to share the gospel of Christ. Some died while on the mission field, and others were never able to return to their beloved Ireland, but they planted churches in distant nations. Because of these Irish saints, the Scriptures were copied and the gospel thrived during medieval times.[2]

When our tour bus pulled into a parking lot at Bangor, we first visited the museum site and then climbed the nearby hill in a public park to pray. The ancient community would have been built there, overlooking the sea. That day the weather was dodgy, shifting between wind, rain, and sunshine, so I pulled out my borrowed fiberglass guitar (it had a great sound and the rain was no problem!) and led the group in worship.

I noticed a friend of mine in the group had been deeply touched by the Lord during worship, and she was a bit teary. When we dismissed for lunch, I asked her, "Would you like to go back to the hill and pray?"

"Yes, I would!" she responded emphatically.

We grabbed a quick bite from a nearby sandwich shop and headed back to the hill at Bangor. A misty rain started to fall, so we slipped under a large, leafy tree to spend a moment in prayer. Suddenly, we both sensed the presence of the Lord. I started playing worship music on my guitar, and we were struck with the realization that thousands of unknown Irish worshipers had given their whole lives in worship to Christ in this place. Their passion to copy God's Word, pray for the world, and worship with their whole heart, even through the bitterly cold Irish winters, was an incredible picture of faith, and this piece of history had left us with a call to action. It was as if saints and angels stood before us, extending the torch of faith, saying, *Now it's your turn! Will you worship, love, and serve the King with passion, as disciples of Christ? Our generation was willing to pay the price to follow Jesus with their whole hearts. What will you do?*

We worshiped and prayed under that dripping tree in Bangor, and my heart was reminded of the ongoing reward of following Jesus: our faith matters, our worship is heard both on earth and in heaven, and we leave a legacy of passion when we follow Jesus with our whole lives. When we choose to be disciples, we become part of a massive tribe that has already done this very thing: run fully after the heart of Jesus and lived radical lives in response to his love. We're not alone in this journey. We're surrounded by a cheering entourage of saints who have finished their race well. The testimony they leave behind reminds us that we too can follow Christ with passion.

> Therefore we also, since we are surrounded by so great a cloud of witnesses, let us lay aside every weight, and the sin which so easily ensnares us, and let us run with endurance the race that is set before us, looking unto Jesus, the author and finisher of our faith, who for the joy that was set before Him endured the cross, despising the shame, and has sat down at the right hand of the throne of God.
>
> Hebrews 12:1–2

Being a modern-day disciple is not so different than it was for the first followers of Jesus. While the context may change, the call of Christ remains the same. *Follow me*, he beckons, giving us the same call that he left the first tribe of believers: *love one another, make time for prayer, give generously, and worship from the heart.*

Just like the early disciples, we'll discover that we're never alone. Jesus is with us, the Holy Spirit comes alongside us, and the living testimony of masses of faithful believers from past ages cheers us on. We discover that we're not just living *for* God but *with* him, surrounded by an audience in heaven that testifies that the rewards are worth the fight. From this place comes a faith rich with meaning that outlasts our lifetime, leaving behind a legacy that impacts others on earth even when we step into eternity. The adventure continues even when we leave this world behind.

May you wrap your fingers around this torch of blazing faith and carry it well, running the race of this life with passion to know Jesus, to love him well, and to love others in his name!

Your Turn

- What is your personal definition of *worship*?
- What are some ways you can implement this in your life?
- Are there new ways to worship that you'd like to implement?
- Define these and explore them!

Spiritual Practice

Write a prayer to God, penning your heart toward him. Include your most honest thoughts, even describing moments in your story that held encounters with him, and thank him for these. As you express your heart, feel free to ask him to take you deeper in worship. Then ask if there's anything he would like to say to you in response . . . a Scripture, his peace, or the simple revelation of his love may come to mind. Thank him, and praise him!

Acknowledgments

Dearest thanks to these fellow adventurers:

Bill and Pam Farrel, my mentors and friends, thanks for cheering so hard for this book! Bill, your help with writing-coaching (and relationship advice) was invaluable. Love you both!

Neil Michael Anderson, my poet-warrior friend, thanks for boldly serving this project and spending hours tirelessly leaning over a laptop with a girl in a cabin, crafting finesse into her wobbling poetry and tweaking her grammar. What a fun journey!

Bill Jensen and Rebekah Guzman, it makes sense that the first steps of crafting this book about divine adventures would begin with our talks on the Oregon coast, with bald eagles circling overhead, and a steady rhythm of waves offering a stunning montage outside the window. Bill, I'm deeply grateful for your assistance as my literary agent, your advice, and your skill as a breakfast chef. Rebekah, it's always a joy to work with you and all the brilliant people at Baker Publishing Group. Thank you both for your energy and belief in this book.

Jamie Chavez, authors often approach the process of editing their manuscript with fear and trembling, but you shattered all stereotypes and made the journey delightful. Thank you for the sensitive, attentive, and even joyous handling of this book. It was a great gift to have you on board as editor.

Patti Brinks, collaborating on this cover with you has been so rewarding. Thanks for the opportunity to share ideas and brainstorm!

Andy, Rolinke, Lauren, and Barbara, what a rich gift to cross your paths on my pilgrim journeys. Your stories add delightful gems to this book. Thank you for living boldly and allowing me to share snapshots of your journeys.

Notes

Chapter 3 Search the Scriptures

1. "Best-Selling Book," Guinness World Records, accessed October 15, 2020, https://www.guinnessworldrecords.com/world-records/best-selling-book-of-non-fiction.

2. Justin Taylor, "An Interview with Daniel B. Wallace on the New Testament Manuscripts," *The Gospel Coalition* (blog), March 22, 2012, https://www.thegospelcoalition.org/blogs/justin-taylor/an-interview-with-daniel-b-wallace-on-the-new-testament-manuscripts/.

3. Truth, Faith, & Reason, "Case-Making 101: How Does the Bible Compare to Other Ancient Documents?," December 4, 2016, https://truthfaithandreason.com/case-making-101-how-does-the-bible-compare-to-other-ancient-documents/.

4. The crucifixion was graphically predicted hundreds of years before this means of execution was even invented. More at https://www1.cbn.com/biblestudy/psalm-22-and-the-passion-of-jesus.

Chapter 4 Community

1. Edith Schaeffer, *L'Abri* (Wheaton, IL: Crossway, 1992).

2. Schaeffer, *L'Abri*.

Chapter 5 Forgiveness

1. Dr. Randy Kamen, "The Power of Forgiveness," *HuffPost*, updated December 26, 2012, https://www.huffpost.com/entry/forgiveness_b_2006882.

Chapter 6 Pilgrimage

1. Wikipedia, s.v. "pilgrimage," last modified October 13, 2020, 10:18, https://en.wikipedia.org/wiki/Pilgrimage.

2. Deuteronomy 16:16.
3. Luke 2:41–49.
4. John 5:1; 7:9–10; 10:22–23; 13:1.
5. Acts 2:1.
6. Acts 18:21.

Chapter 7 Obedience

1. Phillip Keller, *Lessons from a Sheep Dog: A True Story of Transforming Love* (Nashville: Thomas Nelson, 1983), xv.
2. My retelling of the story found in Exodus 5–7.
3. See Exodus 14.

Chapter 8 Meekness

1. Carl Sandburg, in his address at a Joint Session of Congress on the 150th anniversary of Abraham Lincoln's birth on February 12, 1959, quoted in "Lincoln Biographer," Virtual Museum Exhibit at Carl Sandburg Home, National Historic Site, accessed November 7, 2020, https://www.nps.gov/museum/exhibits /carl/lincolnBiographer.html.
2. Joe Wheeler, *Abraham Lincoln Civil War Stories: Heartwarming Stories about Our Most Beloved President*, 2nd edition (New York: Howard Books, 2013), 267.
3. For more information, see David Silkenat, "Surrender in the American Civil War," *History Today*, May 29, 2019, https://www.historytoday.com/miscellanies /surrender-american-civil-war.
4. I never advocate that you stay in or feed unhealthy relationships—meekness is not a "doormat mentality" nor is it an effective means to heal broken people. Any situation with emotional or physical abuse requires clear boundaries and pastoral counsel to deal with.

Chapter 9 Sacred Rest

1. Sarah Klein, "10 Health Benefits of Relaxation," *HuffPost*, April 16, 2012, https://www.huffpost.com/entry/stress-awareness-day-relaxation-benefits_n _1424820.
2. "Shut up and Dance," Walk the Moon, *Talking Is Hard*, RCA, 2014.

Chapter 10 Giving

1. Tracy A. Burns, "Saint Wenceslas (Václav): The Czech Nation's Patron Saint," Private Prague Guide: Custom Travel Services, accessed November 7, 2020, https://www.private-prague-guide.com/article/saint-wenceslas-vaclav-the-czech -nations-patron-saint/.
2. Wikipedia, s.v. "Good King Wenceslas," last modified October 21, 2020, 19:20, https://en.wikipedia.org/wiki/Good_King_Wenceslas.
3. Wikipedia, s.v. "Wenceslaus I, Duke of Bohemia," last modified November 9, 2020, 15:05, https://en.wikipedia.org/wiki/Wenceslaus_I,_Duke_of_Bohemia.

4. Bill Peel, "Why RG LeTourneau Gave 90 Percent," Center for Faith & Work at LeTourneau University, accessed November 7, 2020, https://centerforfaithandwork.com/article/why-rg-letourneau-gave-90-percent.

Chapter 11 Fasting

1. Daniel 10:3.

Chapter 12 Worship

1. Revelation 4:10; 7:11.
2. Ian Adamson, *Bangor: Light of the World* (Newtownards, UK: Colourpoint, 1987).

About the Author

Rebecca Friedlander has been in full-time ministry for nineteen years, ministering both locally and internationally using the creative arts and music. As a film producer, she has created the projects *Celtic Pilgrimage*, *Thin Places*, *Radical Makeovers*, *Pioneers*, and more, as well as dozens of music videos. She has a bachelor's degree in Christian creative arts and leads worship with both original and cover songs, and she speaks internationally with her potter's wheel. When she's not on the road, she enjoys leading personal discipleship and prayer retreats from her father's log home in northeast Texas.

Learn more about Rebecca's art, storytelling, and adventures at
REBECCAFRIEDLANDER.COM

Subscribe to her weekly devotional, read her blog, and much more!

REBECCA
FRIEDLANDER

CHECK OUT MORE OF REBECCA'S FILMS, BOOKS, AND RESOURCES!

To learn more about the films *Celtic Pilgrimage* and
Thin Places and her book *Finding Beautiful*, visit
REBECCAFRIEDLANDER.COM

Bring Rebecca to your next event!
To book Rebecca as a speaker, visit
https://www.rebeccafriedlander.com/booking--contact.html

REDEFINE *Beautiful*

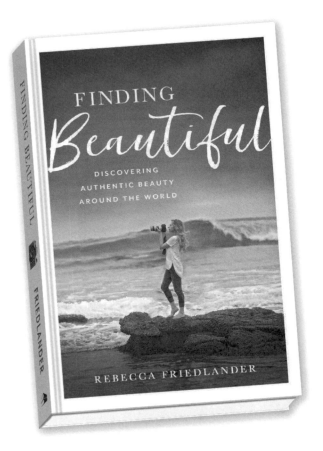

Through engaging personal stories and dramatic before-and-after photography, filmmaker Rebecca Friedlander uncovers the true beauty of twelve women from around the world, empowering us to shatter the lies of rejection, doubt, and low self-esteem.

LIKE THIS BOOK?

Consider sharing it with others!

- Share or mention the book on your social media platforms. Use the hashtag **#TheDivineAdventure**.

- Write a book review on your blog or on a retailer site.

- Pick up a copy for friends, family, or anyone who you think would enjoy and be challenged by its message.

- Share this message on Facebook: **"I loved #TheDivine Adventure by @RebeccaFriedlanderProductions // @ReadBakerBooks"**

- Share this message on Instagram: **"I loved #TheDivine Adventure by @RebeccaFriedlander // @ReadBakerBooks"**

- Recommend this book for your church, workplace, book club, or class.

- Follow Baker Books on social media and tell us what you like.

    f Facebook.com/ReadBakerBooks

    🐦 @ReadBakerBooks